How to Look
for Love

PRAISE FOR *HOW TO LOOK FOR LOVE*

"At last, a relationship advice book that will actually work. If you're intelligent, interested in love, and like a book you can't put down, this is it. John Gray, move over. The brilliant Mari Ruti has arrived."

—Juliet Schor, professor of sociology, Boston College, and author of *Born to Buy* and *Plenitude: The New Economics of True Wealth*

"Why play 'hard to get' when you can just get what you want? Mari Ruti's lively research, from Plato to Freud to *Gossip Girl* to her own bedroom, finally puts an end to playing games and provides a resource for lovers and the love-scorned alike. A must-read for anyone who has ever fallen in love, wants to, or wants to know what went wrong."

—Arianne Cohen, creator of TheSexDiariesProject.com

"As an undergraduate at Harvard, I fell in love with Mari Ruti and her riveting lectures on the highly coveted but frequently misunderstood emotion of love. Countless tomes have been propelled to the bestseller lists by trite tips and tricks on how to find love, but there has been a surprising lack of literature exploring what love actually is and the role it plays in our lives—until now. By affording her readers a comprehensive and enlightening understanding of what the meaning of love is, why the quest for love is so universally important to us, and the purposes that love has in our lives, with this ground-breaking book, Professor Ruti has put the horse back before the cart, opening the eyes of her readers so that they can love better. Whether you're a romantic or repressed, *The Case for Falling in Love* is a must-read for anyone interested in learning more about love!"

—Nancy Redd, *New York Times* bestselling
author of *Body Drama*

"Finally, a book that takes love seriously. The universe is a simple place next to the complexities of love, yet we can't escape a flood of advice offering quick solutions and easy answers. Written with passion and verve, Mari Ruti's book argues that the truth might not be so simple, but ultimately much more rewarding. Love doesn't complete who we are or mark an end to a quest; it opens up possibilities and enables new experiences, if only we are willing to take the risk. I wish I had read this book years ago!"

—Sean Carroll, author of *From Eternity to Here:
The Quest for the Ultimate Theory of Time*

How to Look for Love

How to Look for Love

· · · · · · · · · · · ·

*A Refreshing New Take
on Men, Women,
and Romance*

· · · · · · · · · · · ·

Mari Ruti, PhD

sourcebooks
casablanca

This book was previously published in hardcover as *The Case for Falling in Love*.

Published by Sourcebooks Casablanca, an imprint of Sourcebooks, Inc.
P.O. Box 4410, Naperville, Illinois 60567-4410
(630) 961-3900
Fax: (630) 961-2168
www.sourcebooks.com

Library of Congress Cataloging-in-Publication Data
Ruti, Mari.
  [Case for falling in love.]
  How to look for love : a refreshing new take on men, women, and romance / Mari Ruti.
      p. cm.
  "This book was previously published in hardcover as The Case for Falling in Love."
  (pbk. : alk. paper) 1. Love. 2. Change (Psychology) I. Title.
  BF575.L8R878 2012
  306.7--dc23
                                            2010039642
Printed and bound in the United States of America.
                    VP 10 9 8 7 6 5 4 3 2 1

CONTENTS

ACKNOWLEDGMENTS

These pages would not exist without my super-powered agent, Elizabeth Evans, who had faith that the tiny seedling of an idea that I presented to her would one day be a book. Her intelligent encouragement helped me access a voice that I might otherwise have never found. For this, as well as for her untiring attention to all things large, small, and in-between, I am deeply grateful. If Elizabeth has her kryptonite, I haven't yet discovered it. My editor, Shana Drehs, approached the project with grace, humor, wisdom, and critical edge, helping me improve my argument without crushing my spirit. I thank her for her astute comments and cheerful patience. Sabrina Baskey-East did a marvelous job with the final version of the manuscript, catching a frightening number of blunders—both rhetorical and substantive. Thanks to her, I now know which train station to go to if I want to take a train from Paris to Geneva. Regan Fisher's name cropped up so frequently during the different stages of production that I came to think of her as an invisible sprite who quietly but efficiently kept the wheels in motion.

Numerous friends have contributed their stories, insights, desires, triumphs, and heartbreaks to this book—thank you all (you know who you are)! Special thanks to those male friends who let me quote them in Chapter 2. I can't name them without running the risk of flooding their inboxes with fan mail and marriage proposals, but I feel genuinely blessed to be surrounded by so much masculine decency. Thanks also to Heather Jessup, Miriam Novick, and Jay Rajiva for offering some much-needed comic relief when I was delirious from having overdosed on self-help advice; Jean Russo for her frequent reminders that I wasn't the only one staring at the blank page; Barbara Davis, Barbara Himmelman, and Janet Wells for amiably tolerating my daily anxiety attacks at their quaint library; Anupama Mohan and Suddhaseel Sen for a safe haven, great conversation, and amazing food whenever I needed it; Doreen Drury and Alexandra Gillespie for being unbelievably brave and for always saying the right thing at the right time; Richard Nalli-Petta for designing the beautiful cover; Bohdan Turok for being so stunning that I forgot about the camera altogether; Mary McClung and Corey Law for giving me a way to go on during one of the most painful times of my life; and Marjorie McClung for being such a generous all-American mom.

Finally, I would like to thank the countless smart and motivated students—both at Harvard and the University of Toronto—who have over the years helped me think through the issues presented in this book. I can't imagine my life without your positive energy. Thank you all!

INTRODUCTION

....

MYTH: Learning to read the male
psyche leads to romantic success.

FACT: There's no such thing as the male psyche.

1

I got the idea for this book from a course on romantic love I taught at Harvard for a few years. Truth be told, when I first started to teach the course, I used love as a pedagogical carrot. I knew that my students would be willing to put up with the agony of having to wade through an unusually difficult reading list as long as they got to talk about love. I called the course "On Love: Gender, Sexuality, Identity," confident that the combination of love, sex, gender, and self-identity would speak to young folks eager to find their place in the world.

It worked! The course became immensely popular, drawing an audience from poetry majors to lacrosse players, from purple-haired film students to Gap-clad preppies. Best of all, the more I taught the course, the less love became a pretext for more "serious" topics. I came to realize that love is one of the most soul-sculpting experiences of human existence. It's never just a little piece of life. It gathers and cradles all of life in its embrace, touching the sum total of who we are. When we are lucky, it lends luster to the rest of our activities. When we are unlucky, it spurs us to higher levels of thoughtfulness. Either way, we can't fail. Love is a win-win endeavor, even if it doesn't always feel that we're winning. This is why I'm prepared to make a case for falling in love—why this is a book about the benefits of taking the plunge.

One of the main obstacles to our ability to fully experience the power of love is that most of us have inherited some fairly rigid ideas about men, women, and romance. This is why I made gender such a central theme of my course. I wanted to show that there is a complexity to romance that exceeds stereotypical distinctions between men and women. Not surprisingly, this was the aspect of the course that most energized my students. I discovered that, deep down, many of them were just as annoyed by our culture's dominant outlook on gender as I was. They just didn't have the vocabulary to express their vexation. They sensed that something was wrong, but could not quite put their finger on the problem. My job was to help them do so.

This is also what I'll try to do in this book, for I believe that many of our most basic frustrations about romance are, at bottom, frustrations about gender.

You'll come to see that I'm not a huge fan of our current self-help culture. This culture insists that men and women are radically different. It tells women that to make romance work, they need to learn to interpret the male psyche. This is the first misconception I want to dispel. As a professor of gender studies, I can tell you that there's no such thing as the "male psyche." There's no toolbox of time-tested techniques for luring a man. If the pop psychology section of Barnes & Noble is full of books that insist that such techniques exist, it's not because they actually work; it's because we live in a culture struggling to come to terms with a rapidly evolving landscape of gender. We live in a culture that finds it easier to insist that men and women originate from different planets than to admit that we need to adjust to a new order of things.

This is a book for those who are tired of hearing that men and women dwell in two mismatched emotional universes. It's a book for those who suspect that there may be better ways to approach romance than the gender-specific advice of most relationship guides. If you're a woman who is repeatedly wondering what she's doing wrong with men, you're not alone. Most women I've talked to have asked themselves the same question at some point in their lives. This applies to mature, confident women as much as to young women who are still hovering at the threshold of their romantic lives. The main problem with our self-help culture is that it tends to perpetuate women's insecurity about this. It implies that women actually *are* doing something wrong with men. What I want to do in this book is to liberate you from this mentality. It's a huge drain on your energies. And ultimately it won't get you very far. This is why I'm keen to offer you some new ways to look for love.

2

It breaks my heart to hear otherwise strong and smart women recycle beliefs about romance that belong in the 1950s. When women who are competent in other areas of their lives resort to playing hard to get, massaging a guy's ego, or downplaying their abilities to win the game of romance, something is seriously wrong. Not only does this keep women stuck in the past, but it pits men and women against each other in a battle of the sexes that neither can win. I can't think of anything less likely to produce a good love life than the idea that your partner is an opponent to be defeated. It might have been fun to watch Brad Pitt and Angelina Jolie try to outwit each other in *Mr. and Mrs. Smith*. But unless you're willing to keep a set of military-grade knives in a secret compartment behind your stove, I don't recommend this strategy.

Many women are sick and tired of relationship games, yet keep playing them because they don't see another option. At the same time, many men actually can't stand it when women approach romance with a Mars-Venus mentality. And many emphasize that they dislike it when women hide their true feelings, play helpless, don't return their phone calls, or barter with sex. They understand that this is what women are taught to do. They're not the fools we might want them to be. Their own game, in fact, consists mostly of trying to preempt the game they expect women to play. What could be more paralyzing? Both sides are trying to guess which piece on the chess board the other player will move next. They spend so much time speculating about the outcome of their actions that there isn't much space left for honest feelings. The game, sadly, has come to trump love.

How many relationship guides have you bought over the years? Is your love life any better for having read them? And, most importantly, how do they make you feel about yourself? If you're anything like me, they make you feel that you're not lovable as you are. That to catch a man, you need to bend over backward to fit into a mold that was not made for you (you suspect it might have been made for your grandmother). Worst of all, they suggest that the romantic disappointments you've endured are your own fault. That you keep failing because, despite your best efforts, you always, in the end, commit one of the twelve dumbest mistakes women make with men. Chances are you come on too strong. Or sleep with him too soon. Or let slip that one day you might want to get married. Or ask him if you can leave your toothbrush in his bathroom. Or act too emotional. Or too desperate. Or too needy. Or maybe you cook a dinner that's too elaborate. Or wear a dress that's too slutty. Or reveal that you know how to use the power drill in your basement. Or. Or. Or. The list of false steps that are guaranteed to send a guy packing seems endless. The path to happiness is so narrow—so filled with booby traps—that the only way to navigate it is to let some self-help guru lead you by the hand.

We keep buying these books because we live in a pragmatic culture that tells us that there's little about our lives we can't control. We are taught to streamline everything from our jobs and filing cabinets to how we eat, raise our kids, plan a vacation, and manage stress. There's even an "optimum" frequency to have sex so that we come to feel that we're abnormal if we have too much of it and unhealthy if we have too little of it. As a result, it's not that far-fetched to think that there's a way to turn ourselves from a doormat to a dream girl, from a mouse to a vixen, by changing our dress, speech, body language, and overall attitude. It's not that strange to believe that we can find everlasting happiness by learning to modify our behavior.

Yet there's nothing more antithetical to the spirit of love than the idea that we need to fake who we are in order to attain it. Love changes us, of course. But thinking that we must revamp ourselves before we can be loved can only lead to lowered self-esteem and romantic dead ends.

I don't deny that there are many outstanding guides written by trained therapists and relationship experts that allow us to address specific problems. They may, for instance, help us recognize abusive or commitment-phobic men. Or they may teach us to improve our communication skills. This is extremely valuable. I want to be absolutely clear that my critique is not aimed at such guides. But the kinds of books that give you general advice on how to outmaneuver men don't usually do much more than try to convince you that the way things have always been done in our culture is how they should continue to be done. These are the books that tell you to keep your guy guessing so as to deceive him into thinking that you care less than you actually do. Or they may advise you to echo his opinions so as to allow him to feel manly and important. All of this should make you more than a little suspicious. While traditional gender roles constrain both men and women, women in particular have nothing to gain from preserving the cultural status quo around love and relationships.

3

Clichés about "what men want" and "what women should do to seduce them" reduce the intricacies of romance to oversimplified formulas that can't hold up in the face of real-life complexity. And they make women paranoid. There's a wonderful scene in *Bridget Jones's Diary* that pokes fun at this. Bridget is about to attend a party where she plans to entice the womanizing Daniel (Hugh Grant). She's a nervous wreck and turns to her friends for advice. The gist of this advice is that she should flirt with all the other men in the room, but be sure to ignore Daniel. We laugh because we've all heard this advice before. It's as much a part of growing up female as slumber parties and nail polish. Like Bridget, we know that the advice is silly. Yet we can't help but hope that it might work. We can't help thinking that there's a method to mastering the madness of love.

Yet when it comes to romance, there's no method. There's no correlation between effort and happiness. We can't guarantee the outcome of our relationships by raising our game; we can't keep ourselves from getting hurt by following a set of rules we found in some book. This is why I want to urge you to toss your self-help guides in the closest recycling bin. Doing so will restore to romance the charm, dignity, and courage that it has lost because of all the game-playing. It will allow you, once again, to relish the adventurous spirit of love. And it will help you relate to men in less self-conscious and calculating ways. Not only will you enjoy your relationships more, but you'll also find that men are, for the most part, pretty fabulous creatures. Sure, there are some rotten apples out there—abusive types who hurt and disrespect women. But most modern men are genuinely decent. And they're just as excited about love as you are.

I would say that, at this point in history, the best way to increase our chances for rewarding relationships is to recognize that men and women share experiences of romantic confusion and deep anxiety. Most guys I've talked to feel insecure about love. Most fear rejection. Most are looking for a genuine connection. Most are crushed when a woman they love leaves them. How different is this from how women feel?

Why are many women so ready to believe that men are less interested in relationships than they are? Or that they lack basic emotional intelligence? Why are we willing to listen to authors who claim (for example) that while women are "eerily expert at knowing how someone feels," a man "can't pick up on a sad face until his tie is drenched in his partner's tears"? No doubt you're familiar with this sentiment. But how many men do you actually know who can't tell the difference between a happy face and a sad one? Personally, I know none. And most men I know would be horrified to discover that this is how they're being painted by authors who claim to be relationship specialists.

Relationship guides that endorse outdated ideas about men and women make it more difficult for us to have high-quality relationships. How can we relate to men emotionally if we believe, ahead of time, that they're incapable of understanding emotions? I think we'll do much better if we admit that both men and women mishandle emotions from time to time. And that men, no less than women, suffer when their need for love is not met.

We all desire. And our desire is one of the main causes of our vulnerability. When we are trapped in schemes of relationship manipulation, we may overlook this about each other, with the result that we end up wounding each other much more than necessary. What's more, our efforts to control the course of romance make it much harder for us to experience its full wonder. They make us so cautious—so emotionally wooden and guarded—that they undercut our capacity to feel and express love. The lesson we need to learn, then, is not how to manage love, but how to relax our urge to conquer its inherent unruliness. We need to consider the possibility that the more we try to domesticate love, the more anemic our experience of it becomes.

4

Love is not meant to be controlled. It's not meant to be fenced in. It's not even necessarily meant to make us happy.

Its mission is to introduce us to frequencies of human life that would otherwise elude us. Some of these frequencies are jubilant. Others may feel a bit sad or lonely. What's important, though, is that hitting such frequencies expands our emotional horizons. It releases dormant layers of our being. It adds depth and density to our character, giving rise to more multidimensional futures. When we reduce romance to a bag of tricks, we rob it of its power to transform our lives. We deny that the lessons of love are much more mysterious, much more far-reaching, than anything that could be captured between the covers of a self-help guide.

Falling in love is a lot like slipping on a banana peel: it's sudden and you can get hurt. The difference is that while one clumsy encounter with a banana peel is usually enough to teach us a lesson, the blunders of love don't always sink in as easily. If anything, we tend to repeat the same awkward misstep time and again, until we feel like Charlie Chaplin in a banana grove. In the pages that follow, I'll explain why this is the case. But I'll also show that *the failures of love are not life failures*—that we can't be impoverished by love even when we are bruised by it. One of the greatest things about humans is that getting bruised doesn't spoil us. Unlike plums, apricots, mangoes, or nectarines, humans don't perish as a result of being knocked around by the turbulence of life. This is because we possess the capacity for personal renewal. We routinely replace damaged parts of ourselves with new ones that are, arguably, more resilient, more able to handle challenges. As long as we manage to avoid the trap of growing our skin so thick that nothing gets through, getting bruised can only boost our ability to cope with whatever life throws at us.

To fully appreciate the rewards of love, we may need to revise our perception of what it is designed to accomplish. Many of us are used to measuring the success of romance by its long-term stability. We tend to view all relationship rifts as signs of malfunction. But love has other goals besides durability. I'll demonstrate that there are times when it's better to burn, however briefly, with a reckless passion than to settle into a bland relationship that fails to move our spirit.

I'm not saying that we should actively court instability. Or that security, comfort, and dependability aren't worth pursuing. It's just that if this is how we assess the value of love, we misunderstand its basic vocation. We fail to see that many of life's most poignant insights come to us through the painful setbacks of love. Such setbacks force us to reevaluate the overall direction of our lives. As a consequence, they usually give us something in return for our suffering.

There are situations where it may take a long time— perhaps years—for us to begin to appreciate how we have profited. And some of our love losses never yield gains that are easy to read as such. But I'm willing to bet that if you look deeply enough, you'll find something to honor in even the worst of love's catastrophes. Maybe you learn something new about your needs. Maybe you come to understand your limits—that there are standards of relating that you're unwilling to lower. Or that something that you thought was important actually isn't. Maybe you become better at saying no to hurtful relationship dynamics. Or maybe you find that it's difficult for you to do so. This last scenario hardly seems triumphant. Yet even it grants you a seed of insight that you can put to good use. It tells you something about an important sticking point in your life. If you know how to handle this sticking point, it may become a gateway to something better; it may become an urgent invitation to reassess the blueprints of relating that govern your life.

The difference between love and its close cousins such as infatuation is that, unlike the latter, love always leaves a stamp; it leaves an enduring imprint. Infatuations come and go without asking a whole lot from us. But love is demanding. It asks us to reconfigure our lives so as to create room for its imprint. If our relationship succeeds, we must reorganize our lives to accommodate the person we love. If it fails, we must sort through the ruins—the complex feelings of rage, regret, rejection, etc.—of that failure; we must admit that love's aftermath has effects that we need to attend to. Either way, we have been propelled to a new path, and the road back is forever barred. As difficult as this may sometimes be, it's how human life moves from one stage to the next. In the same way that an untried trail on a hiking trip can suddenly reveal a stunning view, love can jolt us to a destiny that we would have not been able to anticipate. What we make of that destiny is up to us. But the one thing we can't do is to pretend that nothing has changed. Love won't let us. It's stubborn that way. This stubbornness deserves our respect no matter how many times we have bumped against one of its sharp corners. This book is about that respect.

5

While the two halves of this book are related, they have slightly different objectives. If you're someone who has recently experienced a romantic breakdown, you might want to start with the second half. In that part of the book, I draw on my expertise in philosophy and psychoanalysis to address issues related to the repetitive patterns of love, loss and mourning, the character-refining power of suffering, and the rewards of knowing how to let go. This section is written for those who are intrigued by love's incredible power to alter our lives. And it's written for those who are trying to pick up the pieces after a devastating heartbreak. I'll argue that love is such a tangled affair that there's little point in worrying about whether or not you're approaching it correctly. This doesn't mean that you should reconcile yourself to wounding relationships. Lady Gaga's catchy lyrics aside, a bad romance is usually not a good idea. Being able to walk away from one may be essential for your eventual success. But there's also a lot to be said for recognizing that disillusionment is often an intrinsic part of romance.

Moments when love ends badly are valuable turning points in your life. They can lead to important breakthroughs. I'll show you why. And I'll also show you why people who have hit rock-bottom are usually more interesting than people who haven't. So, if rock-bottom is where you find yourself, don't despair! You've been given a rare opportunity to remold your life. You've been given a chance to figure out what you want from your future.

You can't control what happens. But you can control how you *respond* to what happens. In love, as in life in general, the only thing you can control is how you meet what escapes your control. There are times when even this proves impossible—when you're so hurt or overwhelmed that you fail to control your own reactions. That's okay. You're not perfect. There will be failures. There will be embarrassing lapses of nobility. If it's human to err, love is the one area of life where you're most likely to make a fool of yourself. But I'll illustrate that the more capacious your heart, the better you're able to meet the unexpected.

The first half of the book mobilizes my training in cultural criticism and gender studies to argue that old-fashioned self-help advice damages our relationships. It's written for those who are weary of trite generalizations about men and women. I show that the epidemic of books that all give the same advice means that the advice doesn't work. If it did, one book would have done the trick—a long time ago. Most importantly, I would like you to understand that when love goes wrong, it's not because you are unable to meet men's secret desires. It's because love is, by definition, volatile. And, in any case, you're not single-handedly responsible for making your relationships work. Many romance guides imply that you are. But this is a burden you don't want to carry around. It does absolutely nothing for your ability to make good relationship choices. What you need is a man who will accept his share of the bargain—not one who is happy to coast along while you spend your free evenings poring over a stack of books so as to figure out your next move.

This part of the book contains a host of pop culture references I've picked up not only from watching a lot of movies and television shows, but also from teaching courses on gender and the media. Contrary to what you might expect a university professor to say, I believe that television shows and other forms of mass entertainment tend to offer more advanced models of romance than much of self-help literature. Many television shows, for instance, break gender stereotypes much more than they reinforce them. You'll learn that if I had a choice between *Gossip Girl* and the average self-help guide, ninety-nine times out of a hundred, I would choose *Gossip Girl*. Josh Schwartz—the creator of the show (and a fellow Brown grad)—seems to have figured out what most of our self-help docs haven't, namely that young women don't like macho guys. And that young men don't like helpless women. And readers deserve better!

PART I

Changing How We Think about Men and Women

CHAPTER 1

....

Saving the Soul of Love

> **MYTH:** The better you play the game of romance, the more likely you are to secure a man's affections.
>
> **FACT:** Game-playing stifles your unique spirit—the very spirit that the right man is going to find fascinating.

1

Let's imagine you've managed to catch a guy through a meticulous application of the rules of dating that you've gleaned from the self-help guides hidden in your closet. You've kept him on his toes, never returning calls or emails immediately. You've cultivated a mysterious aura of unavailability. Your evenings are so packed that you have trouble penciling him in. You waited three months before you had sex. Even now, you feign a headache once in a while so that he doesn't start to take you for granted. You've never mentioned the M-word. You've dressed and talked in ways that highlight your unshakable confidence. As far as you know, he doesn't think you have any emotional weaknesses. You've learned to flatter him whenever he does something technical (parallel parking is always a good one). And you've become an expert at defusing arguments gently because you know that overtly disagreeing with him will threaten his delicate ego. You've even done what one self-help expert tells you to do, namely to adapt your speech patterns to reflect the class status of your guy. You've learned to say "penis" rather than "pecker." Frankly, this wasn't a major sacrifice. But another piece of advice by the same expert took a good chunk of your pride: You went ahead and found out what your boyfriend liked about his ex so that you can better mimic her. What wouldn't you do for love?

Now what? You're entering the fifth month of the relationship and you realize you're trapped. Either you keep up your game indefinitely. Or you risk disappointing your guy by starting to secrete your own personality into the mix. If you market a self-help fantasy to your lover, you can't in all fairness later resent him for loving that fantasy instead of who you actually are; you can't complain that he doesn't appreciate the "real" you.

Human beings are, of course, so complicated that it's difficult to say what the "real" of any of us might be at any given moment. Yet there's undoubtedly a spirit that is unique to each of us—a spirit that arises from our personal history and captures the distinctive tenor of our identity. This spirit permeates our being, generating a highly specific way of being in the world. It consists of core values and beliefs. And it includes hopes, dreams, wishes, and aspirations. It's subtle, yet we intuitively know when we're expressing it faithfully. We recognize it in the "air" of a candid snapshot. And we sense it in the "aura" that surrounds us during moments when we feel at ease with ourselves.

Treating a relationship like a masked gala kills this spirit; it stifles the energy that lends a sumptuous specificity to your character. And it destroys the soul of love. The whole point of falling in love is that we invite another person to touch layers of ourselves that we usually keep from the world. Love vitalizes us because it activates aspects of our being that normally remain subdued. It targets what is brittle and defenseless. What's so strange about much of the romantic advice aimed at women is that it encourages us to induce men to fall madly in love with us while we ourselves stay unnaturally cool and detached. Somehow we're expected to cultivate an intimate relationship without giving much of ourselves; we're supposed to "love" without caring a whole lot.

This advice is well-meaning. It's designed to ensure that we don't get hurt. But since when has anyone been able to fall in love without taking the risk of getting hurt? Falling in love means that you care. It means that you let yourself feel deeply. That you allow yourself to *fall*—to lose your footing and become slightly disoriented. Obviously, it's prudent to be careful with your heart. But the idea that you should be able to control your feelings while manipulating a man into adoring you makes a mockery of love. It may be a convenient way to plan your future. It may allow you to calculate the pros and cons of a particular relationship. And it may even gain you a proposal. But it has little to do with love. Love, by definition, causes emotional upheaval. Often this is terrific.

Sometimes it's not. But what it can never be is safe. Love asks us to expose ourselves—body, mind, and soul—to a person who matters to us. It asks us to lower our defenses. When we hesitate, it moves on to someone bolder.

Self-help guides that tell us to simulate emotional indifference in order to capture the heart of Mr. Right compromise the integrity of love by turning it into a self-interested quest for a ring on our finger. We're constantly warned that a woman who reveals her attachment risks losing her man. Men, we're told, are predators by nature. They only want what they can't have. Commitment phobia is every man's middle name. Even the most responsive men are secretly afraid of losing their freedom. It's in their blood. They'll ditch any woman who admits to being emotionally hooked. Resistance, then, is the key to your victory. Your best strategy is to pretend that he hasn't as much as scratched your heart. Your most cunning approach is to give him the impression that you've got so many options that losing him would barely make a dent in your day.

But why would you want to date a guy who is scared off by your feelings? I'm not saying you should wear your heart on your sleeve. A degree of reserve can be good, particularly in the beginning of a relationship. You don't want to come across with so much intensity that you'll burn up all the oxygen between the two of you. Your guy needs some space to breathe, for sure. But what's the fun of being with a man who only wants you as long as you keep eluding him?

Undeniably, there are some men who are motivated by the notorious predatory impulse to capture and conquer (more on this in later chapters). But are these the men you should share your life with? Why are self-help books so keen to normalize male behavior that women have always found hurtful? Why are women who are addicted to aloof men deemed pathological while men who run after unavailable women are merely fulfilling their "natural" destiny as valiant hunters? Why has the commitment-phobic man come to represent all men? And why is this guy supposed to be worth our effort?

The worst breakup I ever had was with a man who initially seemed like a carbon copy of Prince Charming. He was kind, generous, attentive, and considerate. I was very happy with him. But I was also a little suspicious: He seemed almost too perfect. So I wasn't entirely surprised when his façade began to crumble. What was beneath was someone utterly different from the guy I had been sold. This wasn't a matter of losing the initial spark of passion. It was a complete personality reversal. He turned out to be the classic commitment-phobe who can't tolerate the deepening of a relationship. This guy sends mixed signals because he can't make up his mind either way. If he can't commit to being with you, he also can't commit to losing you. He vehemently denies wanting to break up with you. But he also can't bear to spend time with you. In his mind, he knows he wants out. But he's too weak to tell you so he starts insulting you in the hope that you'll do his dirty work for him. When you call him on his erratic behavior, he tells you that you're imagining things. Or that you're insecure. Or that you've changed so that he's no longer sure that you're the kind of woman he wants to be with. When you offer him an easy way out, he's mortified. How could you possibly think that he doesn't want you in his life? But then he gets so busy that he blows you off for three weeks. It's enough to drive even the most confident of women a little crazy.

Had I believed the self-help credo that most men are a little commitment-phobic, I might have tried to play a game to hold onto this man. Pretending that I wasn't that invested in the relationship might have prolonged the situation; he might have pursued me longer. But this would have been a tremendous waste of my time. I would have risked becoming emotionally dedicated to a man who not only doesn't know how to commit to a woman, but who, frankly, becomes borderline abusive when he doesn't know how to extricate himself from a relationship that's making him anxious.

This is not unusual. Commitment-phobic men who get nervous when a relationship gets serious routinely start finding all manner of fault with you in order to rationalize their conflicted behavior. They may love you, to the extent that they can. But they also must have a good reason for breaking up with you in their back pocket, just in case they need to play that card. Nothing works better for this purpose than parts of your being that are unchangeable. As a result, they start picking on your appearance or basic personality traits, so that you're suddenly too short, or too tall, or too introverted, or too extroverted. Often the things that now bother them about you are the very things that initially attracted them to you. In my case, the problem was that I was too intellectual. When I reminded him that he had explicitly told me in the beginning of the relationship that he admired this about me, he insisted that I had misinterpreted him—that he had never said any such thing. It was as if Mr. Hyde had suddenly stepped out of Dr. Jekyll's shadow.

Mr. Hyde was a mistake. But I didn't give him enough time to do major damage. I got out fast because I didn't buy into the self-help idea that commitment phobia courses through the veins of most men. I had dated enough other men to know that this guy was an exception. Most men don't mislead you in this way. Most aren't the immature cads that many guides portray them to be. Most are actively looking to build good relationships. And I've yet to meet a man who wants the woman he's dating to pretend to be someone she's not. Generalizations about the "predatory" male nature may offer you some protection against the Mr. Hydes of the world. But they're unfair to all the genuinely loving guys out there. They sell us a version of masculinity that represents the least evolved, the most troubled, subsection of the male population. And they turn flesh-and-blood men into such one-dimensional creatures that we might as well be playing with Ken of the Ken-and-Barbie set.

2

Generalizations about men give us an illusion of clarity. They convince us that we're becoming better at navigating the quicksand of our relationships. But their cost to us can be enormous. They can petrify us, making us skittish about revealing our true feelings. If we're afraid that the slightest sign of emotional investment might cost us our entire relationship, we're unlikely to speak up when something is bothering us.

An example of this that I regularly encounter among my female students has to do with their boyfriends' usage of Internet pornography. While there are women who don't mind this, many are devastated beyond expression. They're not necessarily against porn as such. It's just that there's a difference between being okay with the idea of porn on the one hand and catching your boyfriend using it behind your back on the other. Many women I've talked to feel both humiliated and furious about the latter. Yet they tend to preface their confessions of pain by statements such as "I know I shouldn't care so much," "I wish I could be more confident," "All the guys do it, of course," "I've been told it means nothing," or "I'm sure he still loves me." When I ask them why they don't discuss the issue with their boyfriends, they say that they don't want to nag, crowd him, appear jealous, or come across as insecure. They're afraid that revealing their agony will alienate their men and weaken their already shaky foothold on love.

I find such testimonials hard to take. The issue for me has nothing to do with the ethics of pornography. Different people have different attitudes about the matter. I don't have any interest in arbitrating the rightness or wrongness of it all. But I find it remarkable that so many women accept the idea that what their boyfriends do "on the side" is none of their business—that they don't have the right to ask for sexual accountability. They're so afraid of sending the wrong signal that they're willing to put up with a huge amount of emotional distress rather than confront their partner. Instead of questioning a culture that tends to estimate a man's right to sexual freedom as being more important than the basic well-being of his girlfriend, they blame themselves for not being able to control their feelings of unease, rage, injury, or mortification. From time to time, they even say things like "I wish I could lose a few pounds," "Maybe I'm not giving him what he needs," or "I know I'm not the most attractive woman in the world, so..." Sadly, such statements are not that different from those made by battered women who chastise themselves for their imaginary wrongdoings in order to explain away their partners' hurtful behavior.

It would be unfair to say that self-help literature is directly responsible for women's willingness to put up with wounding emotional scenarios. Much of this literature emphasizes women's right to be treated well and respectfully. Yet it does arguably fortify a culture that tells women that how they feel deep down is less important than how they look and present themselves. It's part and parcel of a social mentality that suggests that there's something shameful about women's feelings. There's a fine line between teaching a woman the "proper" techniques for attracting a man and implying that she's only desirable to the degree that she manages to maintain her poise even when she's hurting inside. And there's a fine line between the widespread self-help notion that men are inherently different from women and the idea that some forms of male behavior, however insensitive, are unalterable (and thus beyond reproach). Self-help advice that instructs women to conceal their feelings paves the way for situations where women would rather resign themselves to their suffering than let show that something is wrong. Why have women's emotions become so demonized?

Men, like women, have the right to decide what they do on the Internet. A guy is entitled to break up with you if he feels that his porn is more important to him than you are. But don't let anyone convince you that he can't stay out of those websites because he's a man. Or that you shouldn't bring up the issue if it offends you. Suppressing strong feelings such as these always has long-term repercussions. It prevents the growth of closeness. And eventually these feelings will find their way to the surface anyway. They'll erupt when you least expect it—when you're past the point of polite negotiation. That's when they really rock the boat.

While I can't tell you whether or not you should stay with a guy who refuses to modify a behavior that's hurtful to you, I can tell you this: You have the right to make an informed decision. You definitely have the right to talk to him about it. Don't let anyone lead you into thinking that your relationship will be better if you learn "to bite your tongue until it bleeds" (to once again quote one of my self-help sources).

3

Living with pornography at the expense of your self-respect is a drastic example. But more "benign" scenarios are easy to find. The problem is not always that we become reconciled to pain. Sometimes it's that we lose faith in ourselves. A few years ago, I reconnected with a friend I hadn't seen for ages. My friend, Nadine, was single at the time. She was full of hope and vitality, just as she had been when I had first gotten to know her. She had a great job that gave her a lot of responsibility. She was daring and self-possessed. Then she started to date a new guy. Not two months passed before the doubts started to creep in. Was she being too clingy? Was she smothering him? Did she make too many demands? Reveal too much of herself? Did she seem too insecure? Too desperate to marry? What did it mean when he didn't call for a couple of days? Was he doing that "man in his cave" thing that all the self-help guides talked about? Or was he silently slipping away? Could we please drive to Borders to see if there was a sequel to that Mars-Venus book she had read years ago?

It turned out that John Gray had written a small library of sequels! Nadine bought *Mars and Venus Starting Over* because she liked the idea of "starting over." On our way back from the store, she anxiously flipped through the pages of the book and chanced upon the following statement:

> In real life it takes a woman time to develop and experience passion. This is not the same for a man. A man

may feel the sexual passion right from the beginning. Men are wired differently. They first feel their sexual attraction, and gradually it develops into affection and then interest. Women are wired to experience interest first, and then sexual attraction. Women are first turned on in their minds.

Oh *no*! *Now* we had a problem. Nadine liked sex. A lot. And it didn't usually take her that long to feel the passion. She had slept with her boyfriend on their second date. And, truth be told, she had wanted to the moment they met. Maybe that was her problem. *She was wired like a man!*

I told Nadine that I also hadn't ever dated a man I didn't want to sleep with from the get-go. And I made a point of stressing that the number one dating complaint of the hundreds of young women I had taught was this very issue. They consistently quarreled with the cultural mind-set that tried to convince them that sex and femininity were incompatible— that there was something wrong with any woman who gave it up too easily. Who knew where Dr. Gray got his ideas? Maybe he didn't like sexually assertive women. Maybe he was talking about women of a totally different generation.

Nadine calmed down. Phew! She wasn't a total freak. There were others like her out there. But then Dr. Gray delivered the really bad news:

When a woman feels sexual attraction right away, it is clearly a warning signal. When starting over, if a woman meets a man who ignites her passion, she should run the other way. When a woman is attracted to finding passion, she lives in a world of disappointment. The only men that make her feel that passion are in some way dangerous...She is automatically attracted to men who can hurt her in some way.

Nadine had read enough. There was no use trying to deny it! She *was* seriously messed up. She wasn't able to resist men who ignited her passion. She couldn't make herself run the other direction in search of someone suitably unexciting. Clearly, she was masochistic, unconsciously soliciting disappointment. Worst of all, her boyfriend had roused her desire. So he was sure to be dangerous. It was just a matter of time before he hurt her!

My irritation at Dr. Gray had no bounds. In a few swift sentences, he turned a healthy female sex drive into a pathology. He translated a cultural double standard about sexuality into an ideal that Nadine—and other women like her—felt the need to emulate. This is perhaps the most disturbing aspect of the Mars-Venus phenomenon. What begins as "description" (men this, women that) quickly becomes a matter of "prescription" (men should, women should). It makes women feel that if they don't fit into the Venus model, there's something wrong with them—that they're somehow badly "wired." Instead of wondering why they should be wired one way or another, they try to find themselves in Venus just to reassure themselves that they are "real" women. Rather than critiquing the fact that our culture demonizes women for sexual behavior that it *expects* from men, they convince themselves that they need to suppress their sexuality in order to attain successful relationships. As far as I could tell, Nadine's boyfriend appreciated her up-front sexuality. But Dr. Gray persuaded her that somehow it was going to be her romantic undoing.

I watched in sadness as Nadine turned from a sexually confident woman to a bundle of nerves. She came to see other women as a threat, wondering if her boyfriend might not secretly prefer a woman who was more inhibited—more "feminine" and reticent about sex. I kept telling her that her boyfriend was unlikely to complain about her not having any major sexual hang-ups. But Dr. Gray's words had incredible power. Bit by bit, paranoia replaced Nadine's characteristic verve. She started to walk on eggshells, relentlessly scrutinizing her boyfriend for telltale signs of betrayal. She analyzed his every mood and gesture, afraid that he might be fantasizing about someone more traditional. She tormented herself about not being "maternal" enough. She considered cutting back her work hours so that she could cook more nutritious meals for the two of them. She bought some new clothes that accentuated her soft side (but also made her look ten years older). She, in short, became so worried about doing her relationship "right" that she lost her spur-of-the-moment playfulness. Over time, the strain of looking over her shoulder made her so tense that her relationship started to feel like climbing Mt. Everest.

4

When something like this happens, it's time to ask yourself, first, if you're with the right guy and, second, if you're unwittingly sabotaging your ability to love and express yourself freely. The second of these questions is as important as the first. You can crush a perfectly promising relationship by placing too much pressure on yourself. This is one reason to give some thought to why it is that so many of us are willing to buy into ideals that war against the realities of modern women. Do these ideals originate from men? Or are we being seduced by the self-help culture that surrounds us? If so, is this culture actually helping us? Or should we start calling it self-hurt culture instead? If you look around critically, you'll quickly discover that romance is the one area of life where women are most likely to let themselves be persuaded that being strong is a bad idea.

Notions of masculinity and femininity have changed rapidly in the last few decades. Traditional distinctions between male and female roles have eroded. Although there are tendencies that persist (so that men are still more likely to become firefighters than women), we know that these tendencies are cultural rather than natural. Few of us would insist that women are inherently incapable of being firefighters, or that men can't be good nurses. We understand that a lot about gender is socially dictated. And many of us recognize that two women can be more different from each other than either of them is from a given man. My friend

Alexandra resembles my friend Jonathan a lot more than she resembles any of my other female friends. I expect that you can find similar comparisons amongst your friends.

Why, then, would you accept self-help notions about how women are supposed to act and how men are supposed to respond (and vice versa)? My sense is that such notions are a last-ditch effort to keep women "in their place" at a time when they have won remarkable victories in virtually every social arena. They are a surprisingly effective means to mollify otherwise fearless women. When all else fails to convince you that you shouldn't fly with the boys, there's always a self-help author to remind you that doing so will hurt your chances of landing a husband.

I'm not saying that self-help authors, as a group, are deliberately trying to keep women down (although there may be some who are). Most of them are genuinely trying to help. And some of them may be relatively unaware of the larger cultural implications of their arguments. Most of them would probably say that they only write what they know women want to hear. Yet what women want to hear is conditioned by what they have heard before—what they have, culturally speaking, been programmed to expect. It's a self-perpetuating loop that can be very seductive for the simple reason that it's familiar to us. It doesn't challenge us in any way. But if we're to change our romantic culture for the better, we'll need to start challenging ourselves; we'll need to push the pause button in order to take a closer look at our most basic assumptions about gender.

One of the most rudimentary goals of cultural criticism—of

the kind of criticism I'm doing in the first half of this book—
is to show that cultures can over time develop unconscious
motivations and belief systems that take on a momentum of
their own. Such motivations and belief systems get woven
into our social fabric so seamlessly that they become invisible to us. Yet they exert enormous power. They are like a
huge spider's web that catches us in its meshes and won't
let us free no matter how much we struggle. And, paradoxi-
cally, what makes this web doubly powerful is that there's no
spider spinning it. There's no one at the helm we can point
to as the culpable party. So when I accuse our self-help culture of circulating hurtful gender models, I'm not talking
about a bunch of self-serving authors sitting in some plush
boardroom plotting the downfall of women. A more accurate
depiction would be to say that they are ensnared in the same
spider's web as the rest of us.

There are those who would argue that this absolves the
authors in question of all responsibility—that their blindness
to what they are doing means that they are mere cogs in a
machine that they can't control. In some ways, this is true.
But I'm inclined to think that authors who explicitly place
themselves in the position of cultural gatekeepers—who
take it upon themselves to tell others how to think and act—
should be self-aware enough to recognize the broader ramifications of what they are saying. They should have the critical
apparatus to be able to detangle themselves from the spider's
web and to see through the conventional opinions that our
culture has come to regard as "self-evident."

I say this because, historically, many of the convictions that our culture has taken to be "self-evident" have been unimaginably cruel and unfair. For instance, there was a time in the United States when it was thought "self-evident" that black and white folks should not eat in the same restaurants, drink from the same water fountains, or use the same bathrooms. It took a serious political upheaval (the Civil Rights movement) to show people that this was wrong—that it was not a "self-evident fact" that black people should be oppressed. Activists such as Martin Luther King Jr. and Malcolm X sacrificed their lives to dismantle prejudices that many people had learned to take completely for granted. Likewise, female pioneers such as Mary Wollstonecraft, Margaret Fuller, and Sojourner Truth taught us to question the "self-evident" notion that women were inferior to men. Thank goodness for their vision and bravery. They had the guts to push the pause button and to force the rest of society to question its assumptions.

Racial and gender discrimination are not the same thing. And I would never want to imply that the romantic troubles of modern women are somehow comparable to the historical situations I've alluded to. Not at all. I am merely pointing out that what societies come to take as "self-evident" facts is sometimes extremely questionable. This is why it's usually a good idea to develop some skepticism about exactly those things that seem most obvious to us. When it comes to men, women, and romance, this is especially tricky because, in this terrain, there is no clear division between the bad guys and the heroes. It's simply not the case that men have all the power and that women are merely the helpless victims of a system they can't modify. Many women actively and willingly participate in the system. As far as I'm concerned, they have the right to do so. If the traditional model suits you, fine by me. Good luck with it! It's just that I don't like the idea that women might fall into this model merely because they think that it's the only one they've got. This is why I'm trying to build toward some alternatives.

5

Let me put it this way. There are definitely some specimens of the conventional manly hunter that persist in our culture. But I wouldn't recommend marrying any of these. They're the kind to insist on belching on the couch while you quietly do the dishes in the background. Whoever is trying to convince you that this is the kind of man you should marry does not have your best interests in mind. Likewise, if you need to play games to retain your boyfriend's interest, it's highly unlikely he's the right guy for you. If his desire wavers whenever you make yourself available, what do you think is going to happen in a couple of years? If he can't tolerate your feelings—if he retreats when you get sad, upset, or angry— why would you want to plan a future with him? If you can't be who you are, or act the way you want, what's the point of being in a relationship?

There are plenty of men who don't need you to play a self-help fantasy. And when the right one comes along, *he'll fall in love with your spirit.* The cliché about love being in the eye of the beholder is true in the sense that what makes you *you* is also what will make you uniquely precious to this man. Men of course admire women who fulfill cultural ideals of beauty and sexiness in the same way that we ourselves may admire certain movie stars, singers, or other celebrities (there are quite a few Hollywood hotties I myself wouldn't push out of bed). But such admiration has little to do with love.

I've often heard male friends admit that even though they appreciate the appeal of some supermodel, they would rather date my quirky neighbor, their best friend's outdoorsy sister, or the punky girl who works at the video store. I confess that, in such cases, I've been tempted to arch my left eyebrow and retort with a sarcastic "Yeah, right, I'll believe that when pigs can fly!" But I also know that when guys say stuff like this, they're expressing something about the mysterious essence of love. They're confirming that love aims at what is specific rather than general and easily replicable. The allure of a supermodel is more general and replicable than the allure of my oddball neighbor. This explains why the supermodel is a supermodel in the first place. She appeals to some common denominator that most of us admire. She will turn heads. She may even gain some dedicated stalkers. But she fails to elicit love (except, of course, from her own partner). She cannot compete with the charm of what is utterly inimitable.

A forty-five-year-old male friend of mine told me recently that when he looks at the wrinkle-free faces of women in the twenty-something category, what he sees is a lack of depth and life-experience. Ditto for the airbrushed models that grace the billboards of the city he lives in. He would much rather date a woman whose face shows the signs of having lived and learned a few things along the way than one who looks like she has stepped out of the pages of *Elle*.

I'm willing to bet that most quality men would rather spend time with a woman who has taken care to cultivate her characteristic spirit than with one who makes all the "right" self-help moves. Such moves may in fact be as ineffective as the wretched pick-up lines that men sometimes resort to. When you deliver a phony "You do that so well, honey" to stroke your boyfriend's ego after he has done a shoddy job at fixing a leak in your kitchen sink, you're not doing anything more advanced than the unfortunate guy who walks up to you in a bar and asks, "What's a nice girl like you doing in a place like this?" We all know this guy needs help. So let's make sure we don't stoop as low. I'm not saying that you shouldn't thank anyone who volunteers to fix your sink. Personally, I send them a bottle of whiskey. But if you find men who approach you with lame pick-up lines awkward, chances are a guy is going to find *you* awkward when you do the equivalent with formulaic self-help advice.

The more you regulate your behavior, the less likely you are to attract the right man. The more you bury your spirit under some self-help game, the more difficult you make it for love to find you. This is because love goes after what is singular about you; it looks for what makes you unique and incomparable. It couldn't care less about your poker face. It wants to penetrate the softest spots of your being. It wants to know what makes you tick and why. It wants to find your top-secret underground facilities. It even wants to x-ray the baggage that you lug around so as to better understand what weighs you down. If you're really lucky, it will offer to carry some of that baggage. It will offer to catch you when you slip.

If you never allow yourself to fall freely, you won't get anywhere near this kind of love. This is why tending the flame that lends your personality its idiosyncratic (even eccentric) zest, edge, or flavor is much more effective than figuring out how long you're supposed to wait until you return a guy's call, cook him dinner, have sex, or introduce him to your friends. And it's definitely more effective than trying to act like his ex. Isn't the ex an ex for a reason?

Our identities are in a constant process of becoming. Who we become depends in large part on the kinds of people we let into our world. Every time another person touches our lives, we become slightly different; we evolve in response to those around us. While every person we meet can potentially become a life-altering influence, no one shapes us more than those we love intimately. As a consequence, it's important that the men we invite into our lives are ones who help us grow in creative directions. In a way, the more complex the men we love, the more complex we become. This is one reason I find much of romantic self-help advice so toxic. It rewards overgeneralizing platitudes that can only bankrupt us. A guy who approaches women as prey to be "conquered"—or who aligns femininity with displays of helplessness—won't do a whole lot for our character; he won't awaken hidden aspects of our being. And he will most likely remain beyond our influence, unable to enter into the kind of emotional give-and-take that brings about mutual transformation.

When you suppress your spirit under some artificial scheme, you suppress the very thing that makes you of interest to a man. In contrast, when you allow yourself to love fearlessly, you release what is most majestic about romance. *You save the soul of love.* Love enthralls you because it ushers you to the periphery of your known universe. Its delicious irrationality defies your attempts to decipher it. It offers no guarantees. You can always make a mistake. You can fail miserably. But that's the gamble you must accept, for you can't have it both ways. You can't fall in love—you can't access the tingling sensation of coming alive—without letting your guard down. You can't experience the miraculous aspects of romance without exposing yourself to its perils. Love breaks you open. It confounds you. Through it, a sliver of magic enters your everyday world. How you choose to care for this sliver is your decision to make. But I urge you not to squander it by buying into self-help fantasies about what makes you a woman worthy of being loved.

....

CHAPTER 2

Men Who Ask for Directions Make Better Lovers

MYTH: Men prefer women who let them take the lead.

FACT: Many quality men are looking for an equal relationship with a competent and independent woman.

1

Let's take a closer look at the gender-specific advice women are given. In some instances, it comes packaged in forms that are almost impossible to resist. Take Greg Behrendt and Liz Tuccillo's immensely popular *He's Just Not That Into You.* The book includes (invented) letters addressed to "Dear Greg" by women in various relationship dilemmas, such as what to do when your boyfriend of ten years still hesitates to marry you. I love this book! I think that Greg's replies are witty, funny, and often genuinely empowering. And I agree with his basic message: Stop making excuses for guys who treat you badly. But then Greg makes one of those unfortunate statements that's hard to brush under the rug: "I'm not advocating that women go back to the Stone Age. I just think you might want to be realistic in how capable you are of changing the primordial impulses that drive all human nature...Men, for the most part, like to pursue women...Remember, you are the catch. They are out to snare you. They are not the tasty little mako that will be so good mesquite grilled in a nice lemon sauce. You are."

I know you're joking, Greg. But are you *sure* you don't (just a little) want women to go back to the Stone Age? And how did you get the idea that woman equals grilled mako past Oprah?

The sad truth is that many self-help guides are bursting with similar statements. The ones penned by women are no different. Sherry Argov, for instance, agrees with Greg in her *Why Men Love Bitches*: "Men are hunters, and like any hunting animal, they are more intrigued by conquering prey when it resists the predator...When a woman chases a man, it has the same effect as if she were to deliver a dead moose to his front door." And despite the spunky girl-power tone of much of her book, Argov tells us that the best route to a man's heart is to let him believe that he's always in control. Women, she argues, should act like the "dumb fox" that secretly runs the show while pretending to be helpless:

> A man needs to feel "manly." That's why he won't stop to ask for directions...If you want him to turn right, tell him "I think it might be to the left." In a man's mind, his navigation skills will always be superior to a woman's. It's all about his ego, which has no direction and no line of rotation.

...

The three words guaranteed to turn any man on? "You are right." You'll never convince him otherwise, so don't bother trying. Let him be right. You be smart. This is precisely the reason the dumb fox lets a man think he's in control. When you appeal to his feeling of power, you "charge up his batteries."

...

A couple of times a week when he's kind or generous, let him know he's the top dog. Make him feel as though he's the alpha-dog and the Grand Poo-Bah. He wears the pants, and he is the man.

...

An obvious "penile" code infraction: When you act too much like Tarzan, he feels too much like Jane. Don't even kill a bug when he's around. Don't change a tire. In fact, don't even change a light bulb. (Heaven forbid, sister.)

Argov ends with this bit of wisdom:

Women who are successful in other areas of life are often the ones who find themselves saying, "I should not have to apologize for being strong." Then the following week they wonder why they "can't find a good man." Because a good man wants a good w-o-m-a-n. .

What century are we in? When you stop to think about it, it's more than a little scary that these kinds of statements are the bread and butter of self-help guides. Authors who wouldn't dream of making a racist joke dish out sexist insult upon sexist insult. And they do so in the name of some supposedly "natural" differences between men and women. They assume—without in any way pausing to question this dubious assumption—that evolutionary biology dictates our romantic behavior so that any attempt to revise traditional gender roles violates nature's "intention." Never mind that if we were stupid enough to follow the dictates of evolutionary biology in other aspects of human life, we might be led to assume that the ancient Egyptians and the Southern slave owners had the right idea because they built societies that, like ant and bee colonies, had a few top dogs and a huge underclass of slaves to keep the system going. We don't do this because we know that the idea is as crazy as it is offensive.

We also don't talk about "natural" differences between different ethnic groups. We know that this is what the Nazis did to justify the Jewish genocide. And what the white slave owners did to rationalize American slavery. We know better than to replicate their idiotic ideas. Why, then, are we willing to listen to self-help "experts" who drone on and on about "natural" differences between men and women?

It's telling that when it comes to understanding the intricacies of the government, the economy, the arts, human intellectual and scientific achievement, or our capacity to make ice cream, we rarely turn to chimps, bluebirds, codfish, or spiders for insight. We know that even if there are superficial similarities between human societies and animal societies, we won't gain much from drawing parallels between humans and other animals. We know that too much evolutionary development stands in the way. But when it comes to men and women, suddenly we're meant to believe that modern women are just like Lucy, the hominoid (named after the Beatles song "Lucy in the Sky with Diamonds") who walked the plains of East Africa more than three million years ago!

2

I forced myself to read a stack of self-help guides in preparation for writing this book. Some of them I had read before, usually after breakups when I had been looking for nuggets of romantic wisdom. But this time around I wasn't reading with my bleeding heart. I was reading with my brain, in the "research" mode I use as a university professor. And let me tell you, the more I read, the more upset I got. Regardless of the good intentions of these guides, their underlying message is that the social gains women have made in the last few decades cause women to fail in love. They—and here's the real bummer—make women fundamentally *unlovable*. Men don't love women who are too competent, we're told. They don't like women who are too intelligent, too ambitious, too driven, too capable, or too ready to take initiative. Don't you dare try to read a map when your guy can't find I-95. Better to die of starvation than to question his navigation skills. And, for heaven's sake, if you're going to change a light bulb, do so when he's not watching. Doing it in front of him will rob him of his manhood. Result? He'll dump you. Ultimately, what he really wants is a w-o-m-a-n who hides her face whenever a little bug crosses the floor (Argov advises women to look away until he has "secured the premises").

Basically, these guides are telling you that the skills that let you shine in your job are your biggest stumbling block when it comes to romance. All the things your forward-looking parents told you about being self-assured will get you in trouble with the opposite sex (somehow the guys you date are much less "with the times" than your dad!). And forget about the idea that today's women can do whatever they choose. This attitude might work in other areas of your life, but when it comes to romance, you'd better keep it to yourself. It (let me say it again) makes you unlovable. After all, as Argov puts it, "a man should feel like Conan the Barbarian a couple of times a week." This may still be a little funny. But what follows definitely isn't: "The classic superwoman wants a relationship in which the man and woman are 'equals.' This is nice in theory, but in practice it becomes a one-sided relationship pretty quickly." So not only does gender equality make you unlovable. It makes you *boring*.

After a few extremely frustrating weeks of reading about how men are biologically "hard-wired" to stray and how women should play helpless to appeal to their protective instincts, I considered my options. I could either book a ticket to a galaxy far, far away from Mars and Venus. Or I could do what Greg Behrendt did to gather information for his book: I could poll my closest male friends. I did the latter, in part because I needed confirmation that my understanding of the contemporary gender landscape was not completely off-base.

Taking my cue from Argov, I emailed my friends and bluntly asked them if it turned them off to catch their girlfriend or wife changing the light bulb. Most of them got back to me with a variant of "What have you done with Mari? Have you lost your mind?" One guy even told me that he was insulted I would ask him the question. What kind of a caveman did I think he was?! I can't include all of their retorts here. You'll have to take my word for it that I couldn't find even one man who thought that his partner's light-bulb changing capacities were a turn-off. Here are some of the more thoughtful responses:

Sean (a scientist and author) wrote:

> Does it turn me off when a woman can change a light bulb? Gag me with a spoon. Of course not. I'm much more attracted to women who are competent and not afraid of showing it. My own lovely wife has a black belt in jujitsu and could break my arm at any

moment, which is much more intimidating than light-bulb changing. And I love it!

I suspect that there are some guys whose masculinity and sense of self-worth are sufficiently fragile that they need to control the traditionally masculine roles—changing light bulbs yes, ironing shirts no. Gender roles exist. But we are past them by now. (I would hope.)

Nick (a grad student who used to surf for the British national team) wrote:

I'm afraid it would be a fairly catastrophic turn-off for me if I found out that my girlfriend couldn't change a light bulb. For me, a huge part of my attraction to a woman is respect and admiration. Competence in anything is one of the biggest turn-ons for me. Frankly, there's little more pathetic in 2010 than a horde of barely-evolved knuckle-dragging men insisting that home improvement, car or bike maintenance, science, engineering, and computers be left as their personal fiefdoms in case they get "emasculated." For god's sake, grow up and, preferably, grow a pair of testes that are not dependent on the relative incompetence of women.

Women have to fight a level of chauvinism that remains at almost absurd levels in most top-flight areas of society. And peer pressure to remain mute about anything other than makeup, clothes, domestic chores, and child rearing continues to aggravate the problem. This all makes women who succeed in resisting these pressures all the more impressive and hot!

Charles (a successful businessman) wrote:

I think it's sexy when women can do stuff. Did you see the *Transformers* movie? There's a scene in which Megan Fox has the hood of her car open, and she's got grease on her face, and she's doing something to the engine. Every man I've heard comment on this has said this was the hottest scene they've ever seen in a movie. Of course, she would look hot dressed in a tent. (In answer to your question: I hate helpless women.)

Josh (the CEO of a major organic food organization) wrote:

I think it's hot when Juliana changes a light bulb. Some of my most favorite time with her is when we do physical work together. Paint. Move furniture. Plant our garden. I've found it really frustrating when, in the past, women I've been with have pretended to be weak or to lack capacity in order to win my affection or support.

In my own brutish, poorly informed opinion, dilemmas in love are dilemmas that are really about ourselves. The dilemma isn't with the other or the pool of others. The question is: What stories and patterns of thought are we willing to give up in order to feel real love and affinity, in order to be alive but also vulnerable? The more I am willing to risk, the more I love. But what do I know?! I've been tentatively dating someone for ten years!

Richard (a lawyer) wrote:

My wife, Alex, is entirely capable of changing light bulbs. But, as you know, she's ambitious and driven. When she's working she can lose herself in the task so completely that she might not notice a burnt-out bulb for days. On those occasions I might be turned on if she asked me to change a bulb. But only because this would mean that she had come up for air—that her sharp focus had softened slightly.

David (a philosopher) wrote:

If a woman revealed to me that she didn't know how to change the light bulb, this would be a sure-fire sign that she's pretty much a moron. In general, I'm not attracted to morons. I'm looking for a woman who is good at the practical skills involved in traveling in remote mountain areas and dealing with avalanche equipment for backcountry skiing. I want to date "a bitch that rips," as my friend Cheryl puts it. I doubt a woman who can't change the light bulb would make the cut.

Andreas (a talented artist) wrote:

The question seems to presuppose that I follow gender roles that predate the invention of the light bulb. It assumes that I understand light-bulb changing as a male activity that if done by a woman necessarily makes her masculine, and that a woman's possible masculinity would be unattractive to me, which would then presuppose that I am only attracted to women who perform a non-masculine femininity. None of this makes any sense, and is way too confusing. So I suppose that I would prefer the two of us to just sit in the dark.

Michael (a brilliant journalist) wrote:

Interesting question. A little personal, methinks. If the answer is "no," does that mean I'm comfortable in "The EZ" (The Emasculated Zone)? That wouldn't be good, would it? I wouldn't want the world to know that, would I? So maybe I shouldn't mention that the reason she changes the bulbs in our cozy little lovers' cottage is because I can't do it right and she can.

I guess at the end o' the day, I can fall back on

the words of the Creator, when She said in Genesis,
"Let there be light, dammit! We've got a burned-out
bulb! Do I have to do everything around here all by
Myself?!" In other words, the wife and I are way past
the old "Hey, let's screw in a light bulb so we can get
it on" sex games. That's so utilitarian. So "B" movie.
We're on to the lawn mower now.

There you have it, straight from the horse's mouth. The
only thing to add is this true story: Michael's wife Jean emailed
later to say that the moment I was having this exchange with
her husband, she was driving from the grocery store with
four new light bulbs on the backseat of her car. Which leads
me to wonder how she has managed to hold on to Michael
for their fifteen-plus years of marriage. She's one of those
women who gets genuinely excited when someone asks her
to assemble a piece of IKEA furniture. And whenever I buy
a new laptop, I bring it to her house because I know that
she'll be able to turn it into the glorified typewriter I want.
So I know that Michael hasn't hung around because of Jean's
technical inaptitude. But it might have something to do with
the fact that she can rattle off the batting average of every
major baseball player in the nation.

3

What have we learned? That men love strong, competent,
intelligent, light-bulb-changing women. Some of them even

want you to know how to handle avalanche equipment—which I admit is a little intimidating.

Obviously, I didn't conduct a scientific study. I know I have cool male friends. I knew when I sent out my question what kinds of answers I would get. My point is not to say that all men feel the way my friends do. I will, however, insist that my findings are no less valid than those of Greg Behrendt and Sherry Argov. What you find depends on who you ask. And how you ask them. If I had asked my friends if they feel good about helping a woman get a heavy suitcase out of an airplane overhead compartment, most of them would have said yes. This is because they are *nice* people. But if I had asked them if they get turned off by seeing a woman manage it herself, they would have said no. This is because they are *sane* people.

Let's say I'm conducting a survey on how men feel about being asked out by a woman. And let's say that my question is: "If you meet the hottest woman you've ever laid eyes on and she asks you out, will you refuse her invitation because you want to be the one doing the asking?" You would have to be a fairly dim bulb to say that you wouldn't go out with this woman (unless you're attached, of course). But what if I phrase my question as follows: "How would you feel about the wild-eyed woman you couldn't shake at a party tracking down your phone number and calling you eight times a day to ask you out?" We all know what the answer would be.

Granted, most self-help authors conducting "polls" won't resort to anything this extreme. But the point stands: How you frame your questions about men, women, and romance shapes the answer you get. As does your pool of respondents. If you're a couples counselor who writes a book based on what you have learned about men by conducting therapy for twenty years, of course you're going to say that men suffer from intimacy issues, autonomy issues, communication issues, and commitment issues. That's because the men you see in therapy *do* suffer from such problems. That's why they're in therapy. But this doesn't mean that all (or even most) men have these problems.

Not all men are like my friends. But not all are *unlike* them either. The "men" you read about in self-help guides—the ones who don't want you to change the light bulb—are no more representative of "all men" than are my enlightened friends. I've only ever been able to track down one or two of these boorish types. Dunno. Maybe they see me coming and run for cover. But it's more likely that they are a figment of our collective imagination—something concocted for our benefit by self-help authors who embezzle each others' ideas with abandon. Their thoughts have a life of their own in the sense that once one author(ity) swears by a given insight, others immediately follow suit. They hand out sexist diatribes like Halloween candy. But let's place blame where blame is due. We gobble down this candy. We devour the last morsel of it. We steal it from the mouths of unsuspecting eight-year-olds. See that little girl in a fairy costume? Is she hiding a Snickers bar? And then we complain about having a stomach ache. When it comes to bad diets of self-help literature, we truly are our worst enemy. I've never seen a guy walk a woman to the pop psychology aisle of Barnes & Noble, hold a gun to her temple, and say, "Buy one of these or else..."

Joking aside, listen to what my friends Bohdan and Charles have to say:

Bohdan (a therapist and gifted photographer) wrote:

> Men are hard-wired to cheat? How convenient! And how scary for the woman. And, yes, I love to "protect." How else can I feel like a manly man?! I understand why you would want to combust. I'm just imagining a relationship based on this advice and can't help but envision a parody. It turns the woman into a victim of her own device. She traps herself in the circus of her own trickery. The man then becomes a beast that has been trapped and deceived into intimacy and fidelity. Nice.

Charles (the Megan Fox–lover from above) wrote:

> The one huge advantage men have over women is that men do not subject themselves to the endless deluge of ego-killing, confidence-undermining trash that women do. *Cosmo?* What more effective tool of female oppression has there ever been??? Why do women agonize so much? They have all the power, until they give it away by second-guessing themselves so much!

For all the manipulating they do, and are taught to do, women are sucked into societal norms that equate manliness with traits that are actually bad for relationships—machismo, silence, stoicism, etc. Men are as desperate for relationships as women are. If women would just stop plotting to "entrap" some unavailable jerk because unavailability is considered masculine, they would have their pick of guys who would be grateful for the chance. Unfortunately, women have been taught that men who are available must be defective.

Bohdan and Charles have a point. The more deeply you walk into the self-help trap, the more likely you are to fortify your own prison. You may think that playing helpless will give you a romantic edge. But, actually, all it does is to weed out the egalitarian men. Consider the idea that women should let men do all the initiating in relationships. This right away rules out any guys who might have all-too-human insecurities about their desirability. What you're left with are the aggressive jerks who like to dominate women. You're left with the cocky macho types who love the thrill of the chase. Or the players who are more than happy to pick up a woman from a lineup at your local bar. In other words, the very men who are good at the first move may not be that good at building a complex emotional bond. They may be exactly the guys you should most watch out for.

4

This is where Greg Behrendt and I disagree. Greg desperately wants women to wait for guys to ask them out. In his words, "Just because you like to lead doesn't mean he wants to dance. Some traditions are born of nature and last through time for a reason." There we go with "nature" again. Greg, what do you know about nature? Don't you live in LA?

I of course understand that there are guys who like to take the lead. There's nothing wrong with that. But I also trust that men who can handle an independent woman can handle being pursued a bit. Conversely, I'm not totally convinced that every guy who is interested in me is going to be willing to fight a dragon to show it. Greg tells me that any guy who doesn't call me first, scour the phone book for my number, harass me sexually, stalk me, pick up the dinner bill, or declare his undying love within the first few months just isn't that "into" me. A guy's busy at work? Not that into me. He has an important deadline? Not that into me. He needs to take things slow because he just got out of another relationship? Not that into me. He has issues he's trying to work through? Not that into me. He's slow to propose? Definitely not that into me. His grandmother died so he forgot to call me on Sunday? What am I waiting for?! Lose the bastard already!

Let's give Greg some points. He does understand about the guy with the dead grandmother. And he's right that if a guy doesn't return my calls, never initiates contact, prefers to sleep with other women, or runs the other direction when he spots me on the street, chances are he's not that into me. Obviously, I don't want to lavish my energies on a guy who isn't willing to make me a priority. I get that. Absolutely. And I agree that if I find out that a guy isn't that into me, I shouldn't waste my "pretty" (as Greg puts it) on trying to win him over.

Greg's probably also right that if my relationship ends, there's no point in racking my brain for explanations. There's no point in dwelling on what I should have done differently. Or what the guy's "issue" might have been. The brutal truth is that he probably just didn't dig me enough and moved on. It wasn't meant to be. That's hard on the ego. But it frees me to look for a man who appreciates what I've got to give. I'm with Greg on all of this. But can we please get there without the creepy gender stereotypes?

In Greg's gendered universe, all is well when men take action and women respond. Men compete for women. Women are the trophies that men "win." Men wound. Women get hurt. Men hold power and make decisions. Women meekly (and breathlessly) wait for these decisions. Men are unemotional. Women are emotional. Except co-author Liz Tuccillo. Liz admits that she hates talking about her feelings: "I know I'm a chick and chicks are supposed to be all emotional, but I'm not." Hmm. *Interesting.* Does the fact that Liz doesn't feel the way chicks are "supposed" to feel make her crazy? Or might there be something wrong with the idea that there's a standard, one-size-fits-all "chick-way-of-feeling"? I would give Liz the benefit of the doubt. I don't think she's crazy. What's crazy is the idea that all women are supposed to be this way or that.

According to *He's Just Not That Into You*, the worst thing a woman could do is to show any initiative. In fact, the tiniest glimmer of assertiveness will haunt her for the rest of her life. If she's stupid enough to marry a guy who failed to call her first, she'd better start counting the days to her imminent divorce. Because, eventually, he'll realize that *he* should've been the one to pick up the phone.

In the movie version of *He's Just Not That Into You*, we're meant to believe that the marriage of Bradley Cooper and Jennifer Connelly collapses because Jennifer pursued Bradley in the initial stages of their relationship. We're meant to believe that Bradley falls for Scarlett Johansson's charms primarily because Jennifer made the first move more than a decade ago. The erosion of passion after years of married life has nothing to do with it. Nor do Scarlett's considerable assets. It's all about the fact that Bradley didn't get to be the man in the relationship's prehistory. *As if.* Bradley Cooper is better than that.

All things considered, though, the movie version of *He's Just Not That Into You* is much better than the book. This is because it emphasizes—in a way that the book doesn't—that when the right person comes along, our usual expectations about who is supposed to do what during courtship disintegrate into a heap of dust. The movie ends with Justin Long's self-satisfied character admitting that Ginnifer Goodwin— the pathetic girl who has made a fool of herself throughout the movie by pursuing guys who are not that into her—is his true love or, as he puts it, his "exception." He has spent the entire movie instructing her on the "correct" ways to handle men, only to reveal in the end that, when a guy truly likes a woman, it makes absolutely no difference that she has broken every rule in the book, including the one that tells women never to initiate sex. After all, this is the woman who a few scenes earlier pinned him to his couch and covered him with unsolicited kisses. Thankfully, the final message of the movie is that when it comes to your "exception," you're willing to push aside the gender codes that you might usually navigate by. This is excellent news, not the least because the person you fully fall for is, by definition, *always* your "exception." Right?

5

You won't find your dream guy on the pages of your average self-help guide. That's where the knuckle-dragging hunters congregate. And what's so strange is that the authors of these books seem hell-bent on us dating these knuckle-draggers. For reasons that escape me, many of them seem to believe that we should be *happy* dating macho guys. That we should *like* it when guys refuse to stop for directions, insist on being the ones in control, flex their egos, or grunt when we try to talk about our feelings. Or maybe it's that these authors think that these kinds of guys are the only ones out there—that we don't have a choice? Is it possible that what I'm calling a knuckle-dragger is, for them, simply an average guy? If so, I must be living in some alternate universe because I honestly don't know any men who think that stopping for directions is a major blow to their ego. (I do know one woman like this, though.)

To Greg Behrendt's credit, the only thing he's insisting on is that the guy take the lead. Otherwise, Greg recognizes male stereotypes for what they are, namely excuses for bad behavior. As my friend Bohdan so astutely noted above, there's nothing more "convenient" for men than to believe that they're "hard-wired" to cheat. This lets them off the hook when they do something horrible like sleep with their ex behind your back. Likewise, if a guy wants to skip out on you without an explanation, commitment phobia comes in pretty handy. And if he's too selfish to deal with your emotions, what better way to slide out of having to make an effort than to claim that men don't "get" feelings?

My point is that men who fit the template of traditional masculinity are much more likely to exploit women than more egalitarian men because they, quite simply, think that they have the right to do so. This is why I would much rather date guys who ask for directions than ones who don't. Such guys know that their navigation skills are not infallible—that they can't always get things right the first time around. And because they're not afraid to pull up to the nearest gas station, they're much more likely to find the highway than guys who insist on going on aimlessly. The happy-go-lucky wanderers will exhaust you ("Enough already," you'll want to scream). In contrast, guys who stop for directions tend to be the clever type. When they find themselves at an intersection that confused them before, they'll want to improve on their performance. By the time the macho guy starts thinking about finding a map, one of these overachieving types will have ushered you to your destination multiple times. He might have even insisted on taking the scenic route—the one recommended by the gas station attendant. And, because your driver is a considerate guy, he will have taken care to drive carefully so as not to make you carsick (OK, he also didn't want you to puke all over his Porsche).

My advice? If you have a choice between a guy who is too proud to admit that he has missed his turn and another who isn't scared of the Exxon sign beckoning by the roadside, don't hesitate to opt for the latter. He's much less likely to disappoint you than the guy who insists that it's his "natural" right to lead even though he doesn't have a clue about where he's headed.

CHAPTER 3

....

·Bad Science Can't Tell Us a Damn Thing about Love

MYTH: The key to human romantic behavior lies in evolutionary biology.

FACT: Human love is as different from animal mating as Shakespeare's sonnets are from chimp language.

1

I mentioned that many self-help authors who perpetuate gender stereotypes believe that men and women are inherently different. Such authors routinely fall back on evolutionary models, arguing that the key to male and female behavior resides in biology. Sherry Argov puts this brusquely when she asserts that the truth about men can be found on the Animal Channel. Even though scientists, sociologists, and psychologists routinely report that differences *among* men (and differences *among* women) are more significant than differences *between* men and women, popular writers can't seem to shake the belief that men are closer to (male) chimps than they are to women. In a culture where there's nothing worse for a guy than to be thought "feminine," relationship experts are doing their best to convince us that if it really came down to it, men would rather cast their lot with the manly baboons than with human females.

News flash to those who insist that men are biologically programmed to hunt women: When male predators (say, leopards) go hunting for food, they don't target females of their own species. They chase zebras, gazelles, antelopes, and water buffalo. But they are not stupid enough to pursue their own potential mates.

Let's examine the evolutionary biological model of romance. I seem to stumble upon a crop of guides that advocate this model every time I'm killing time at some airport newsstand. During a recent layover in Chicago, I came across Leil Lowndes's promising title: *How to Make Anyone Fall in Love with You*. For some reason, the store was filled with stacks of this book so that the only way to avoid it was to retreat to the pin-up periodicals of the "men's interest" section. Ironically, when it comes to holding onto your dignity, you might be better off reading *Maxim* than this book. It boldly declares that scientists have finally, at long last, solved the secrets of love. And it outlines eighty-five techniques (built on "a solid scientific base") that are guaranteed to make a man fall in love with you. Never mind that Lowndes has no scientific training. Or that the book's methods aren't scientific by any stretch of the imagination. Or that the "research" cited includes obscure gems such as a 1952 study of the impact of lipstick on first impressions.

The book painstakingly outlines every step of the dating

process, from how to dilate your pupils, adjust the tone of your voice, and soften your body language to how to "manipulate" a man's sexual fantasies. It's a toss-up as to what makes this guide more agonizing: Its conviction that, starting with the first date, your quarry "looks at you through the eyes of an Olympic judge" so that everything you say and do "can give you points or ruin your chances at the gold medal"? Or its enthusiastic endorsement of the worst gender caricatures of our culture? The following tip aimed at men is representative: "Palms up is an excellent sign. Hunters, when she has her palms facing you, it means she likes you. She is feeling vulnerable and probably welcomes more closeness. Palms up is the classic 'I submit' position." Speaking to women, Lowndes adds: "Does your Quarry shake a finger in the air while making a point? Think of a pointed finger as a mini erection which shows excitement over a particular detail... Take it as your cue to express your wholehearted agreement with him."

At the risk of sounding like a broken record, I've got to ask again: What century are we in? Besides the obvious wobbliness of "science" such as this, what's so troubling about these statements is the deferential role they give to women in the dating game: Women are to "submit" and to respond to a guy's pointed finger by "wholeheartedly" agreeing with him. The book is an extreme example of the tendency of self-help guides to turn conventional cultural beliefs into "scientific" facts. Such guides strive to prove the "objective" validity of some of our most worn-out attitudes about gender. The problem is that, with some fine-tuning, you can make "science" confirm just about anything you want.

As I already pointed out, it all depends on how you frame your hypothesis and go about conducting your research. Professional scientists know this, which is why most of them are careful about not introducing social tradition into their research findings. They do their best to conduct controlled (and repeatable) experiments under conditions that have been stripped of all cultural influences. The more their results resemble cultural clichés, the more suspicious they get because they know that this may be a sign that they have not been able to divorce their experiments from social prejudice (science being the very antithesis of prejudice). Not so with a lot of self-help experts. Many of them appear to view science primarily as a convenient way to lend credibility to convictions that are based purely on man-made customs. Not all of these convictions are false. But when it comes to habitual beliefs about men and women, it's wise to question their reliability. If we hadn't learned to do so, we would still be wearing chastity belts and pretending that we don't know how to calculate 15 percent of a hundred dollars.

No writer has done more to popularize the "scientific" approach to love and relationships than Helen Fisher. Fisher is an anthropologist—an academic with impeccable credentials. Her 1992 *Anatomy of Love* is a classic in the field. And her more recent books have had an enormous impact on how we, as a culture, envision romance. To Fisher's credit, much of her work aims to dismantle the nastiest of our popular misconceptions about "natural" differences between men and women. She explains that, in many animal societies, it's the females that hunt. And animal females are rarely the passive wallflowers they are made out to be in the popular imagination. Female chimps, for instance, initiate sex up to 85 percent of the time. And once they get going, they are likely to copulate with as many males as they can get their hands on. So much for the idea that men are programmed to seduce women and initiate sex. And so much for the idea that promiscuity is somehow more "natural" in men than in women.

I hate to burst the bubble of those men who think that it's their natural birthright to stray while women are designed for monogamy and faithfulness, but here it is: The more one believes in evolutionary explanations, the more one is forced to admit that women are as likely to sleep around as men are. Fisher speculates that the double standard that allows men to cheat while vilifying women for doing the same is a relatively recent invention—something that came into being in agricultural societies where women became pawns in elaborate systems of property exchange. In such systems, women's value depended on their purity, which meant that their sexuality became strictly monitored. Female sexual "coyness," according to this account, has nothing to do with nature. It's a social fabrication.

2

Fisher does us a huge service in shattering some of our most entrenched stereotypes. But this is not enough for me. I'm fundamentally suspicious of attempts to explain human romantic behavior through biological models. Such attempts have historically almost always been used to convince us that there's something "natural" about gender inequality. I don't deny that biology plays a part in attraction. I know that brain chemicals are important, as are hormones. And I know that we go through physiological changes whenever we experience strong emotions of any kind. It's just that I get a little jumpy when a scientist argues that "people probably began to discuss attraction more than a million years ago when they lay on riverbanks in Africa to rest and watch the sky." I'm no scientist. But I do know that the line between science and science fiction here is razor-thin. Or let's take the following insight from Fisher:

> Love at first sight. Could this human ability to adore another within moments of meeting come out of nature? I think it does. In fact, love at first sight may have a critical adaptive function among animals. During the mating season a female squirrel, for example, needs to breed. It is not to her advantage to copulate with a porcupine. But if she sees a healthy squirrel, she should waste no time. She should size him up. And if he looks suitable, she should grab her chance to copulate. Perhaps love at first sight is no more than an inborn tendency in many creatures that evolved to spur the mating process. Then among our human ancestors what had been animal attraction

evolved into the human sensation of infatuation at a glance.

The lesson here is that if I want to have a child, I shouldn't have sex with a porcupine. But in principle any reasonably suitable guy should do. I should be willing to have sex with most of the world's male population. I would weed out the ones with "inferior" genetic material, of course. But I would still have a lot of possible targets. In any given subway car, I should find at least twenty guys I want to sleep with. Sad to say, this is not the case. I can go for six months without meeting even one guy I'm dying to shag. If the subway cars of your city yield a better sample, please let me know where you live so I can start packing my bags.

And what about this little detail? Whenever I have sex, I do everything in my power not to produce a baby. If my desire to have sex arises from my innate drive to have babies—as evolutionary biology tells us—why is it that I've spent vast amounts of money trying to keep myself from accidentally bringing one into the world? Come to think of it, the only times I ever refuse sex (when the guy is right) are those when I can't *guarantee* that a baby won't follow. I don't say no to sex because I have a headache, or because I'm too tired or stressed-out. The only two things that will keep me from having sex (with the right guy) are food poisoning and the fear of inadvertently producing a baby!

Human desire is nothing like animal instinct. And human sexuality has little to do with reproduction. Although there are times when people have sex in order to reproduce, sex and babies often don't line up. While animals have sex primarily to conceive, humans have sex for all kinds of reasons, for instance to express love, to build intimacy, or to experience pleasure (or even transcendence). Women frequently have sex when they are already pregnant (or when they are too old to bear children). And folks who are trying to conceive a child routinely have a lot more sex than would technically be necessary for the task. Biologically speaking, if you want five children, you might only need to have sex five times in your entire lifetime (provided you time yourself well and do not have any problems with conception). The fact that this is not how most of us go about our sex lives reveals that while reproduction is obviously a component of human sexuality, it plays a relatively minor part. And for some people, it plays no part at all.

What's more, there's an almost frightening specificity to human desire that can cause a lot of frustration. I'm not the only one who can't find twenty sex mates every time I step into a subway car. I have three male friends who look like Calvin Klein underwear models. These men can melt butter with a glance. Yet two of them are pining for women they can't have. And the third has confessed that before he found his current girlfriend, he spent years—and I really mean *years*—looking for a woman to date. He tried everything from bars to blind dates to eHarmony.com. It's hard to know what the problem is. These are guys who are fending women off with a stick. Hell, I'm upset they won't sleep with *me*.

As empathetic as I try to be when they go on and on about the shortage of suitable women, in the back of my mind I'm saying, "What's wrong with me? If you were more like those bonobo chimps that the evolutionary biologists keep talking about, you wouldn't be so damn discriminating."

When it comes to sex, most people are astonishingly discriminating. And our desire can be annoyingly stubborn. Often it fixates on a person who won't give us the time of day. Even when there's virtually no encouragement, our desire can circle around a specific person until we get so aggravated that we move to a different state. Where's the Darwinian advantage of this? What evolutionary purpose can it possibly serve? If the goal is to produce babies, I can't think of anything less efficient than courting a person who refuses to have sex with us.

One of my favorite moments in *Anatomy of Love* is when Fisher tries to give an evolutionary explanation for the fact that women often have sex without any intention to reproduce—and that they are as likely to stray as men are. When it comes to men, promiscuity makes evolutionary sense because men are supposedly programmed to spread their seed as widely as humanly possible (could someone please tell my CK friends?). But what about women? What evolutionary reason could there be for straying? After all, women can only have one child (or a handful at best) at any given time.

Fisher patiently explains that a woman might stray because she's trying to secure favors from as many men as possible. If she's anything like female chimps, she's trying to confuse paternity so that each male in the community will act generously toward her and her babies. And—get this!—she's trying to keep the males in her troop from killing her babies. By this reasoning, if I'm a suburban soccer mom, I would do well to sleep with half the guys in my tree-shaded neighborhood because, that way, they won't kill my children!

Obviously, I exaggerate. I know that there might be ways to spin Fisher's argument to make it more applicable to contemporary life. Maybe the woman who sleeps around simply wants her male neighbors to take her son to the zoo. Or to wash her car once in a while. I actually know a woman who swears by this strategy. She makes a point of always having more than one boyfriend on a string, so that one will pick up her groceries, another will drive her to the airport, and yet another will water her lawn while she's out of town. The problem, of course, is that she also has to keep these guys from killing each other. As far as I can tell, it can get pretty exhausting at times.

I'm also being a little unfair to Fisher. I know that she's not positing a direct link between female chimps and human women. Rather, she's arguing that women carry an evolutionary "imprint" of the reproductive imperatives that dictate the behavior of chimps. This same imperative also ensured the survival of the proto-humans that roamed the earth four million years ago. So when you sleep with a coworker at your company's New Year's Eve party, you're not necessarily consciously trying to produce a baby. You're probably not even trying to keep the guy from murdering your already existing children. Instead, your behavior is unconsciously motivated by a biological imprint that has been passed on over millions of years of evolutionary development.

I suppose that either you buy it or you don't. I don't.

3

The reason I don't buy it is that even if such an imprint existed, there would be no way to separate it from all the social forces that condition our sexual and romantic behavior; there would be no way to isolate the biological imprint from all the cultural messages that surround us. Gender indoctrination—otherwise known as socialization—begins well before we pop out of the womb. If the parents know that the child is a girl, they'll paint the nursery pink. If they are "modern," they might choose another color. But it's unlikely to be light blue. And friends and relatives start bringing frilly little frocks, cute little dolls, adorable little stuffed animals, and miniature tea-party sets (note the emphasis on "little"). They'll shy away from model railways, squalling fire engines, toy soldiers, and chemistry sets. But what if the doctor's office made a mistake and out comes a little boy? Wouldn't that be a catastrophe!? You would have to repaint the room and return all the gifts.

One of my graduate students, Christina Konecny, wrote a brilliant term paper on how the physical layout of preschools socializes boys and girls into gendered behavior. Apparently, many preschools have something called the "home" area. This is often stocked with dolls, cribs, blankets, strollers, brooms, dustpans, household appliances, sponges, used food packages, cookbooks, dishes, and a child-sized kitchenette complete with sink, stove, and refrigerator. This area is geared toward intimate play. It's often praised for being essential for emotional development. Girls mostly play in this area.

Boys, in contrast, dominate what's called the "block" area. This is an open, carpeted space that contains toy cars and trucks, building materials, games and puzzles, and (sometimes) "dress-up" clothes such as firefighter or policeman hats. If the home area is the "private" space of the preschool—the space where girls learn emotional, maternal, and interpersonal skills—the block area is the "public" space where boys learn the rules of collective action, along with important spatial, conceptual, organizational, and managerial skills (such as the ability to lead others toward achieving some shared goal). Christina points out that despite the common assumption that children are free to choose where they play, there's little doubt that the home space is coded as being "girly" and that, consequently, few boys opt to play there.

I find this chilling. Yet preschools are only one of the many arms of gender socialization. Think of how parents talk about their children. Though it is these days acceptable to hope that one's daughter becomes an accomplished doctor, lawyer, professor, or business executive, most parents don't like the idea of their sons being fond of ballet, needlepoint, lacy curtains, Jane Austen, or picturesque sunsets. It's not that parents consciously seek to brainwash their children. It's just that gender-specific directives are so common in our culture that it's almost impossible for anyone to escape them.

Children, adolescents, and sometimes even adults get ridiculed and punished whenever they deviate too far from what is expected from boys and girls, men and women. The boy who is bullied on the schoolyard for being a "sissy" is unlikely to grow into a man who coos at babies in public places. And the brainy teenage girl who gets branded as an ugly duckling with no romantic prospects will quickly learn to hide her intellect under a "girly" veneer of sweet compliance. She may even choose to spend her evenings practicing putting on makeup rather than cramming for her physics midterm. When she does badly on the exam, people will tell her that it's because she's a girl. After all, everyone "knows" that boys are better at science than girls.

The French philosopher Simone de Beauvoir famously states that "one is not born a woman, but becomes one." What she means is that none of us enters the world with an instinctive understanding of what being a woman means. We gather this understanding gradually, through being immersed in a cultural environment that holds particular views about men and women. We begin to learn how to correctly "perform" our gender well before we learn to speak. By the time we are adolescents, the codes of appropriate femininity are so deeply ingrained, so automatic, that we consider them as innate. We don't recognize them as cultural constructs, but rather take them to be an accurate reflection of our "nature"; they are simply who we "are."

Cultural constructs are incredibly compelling. Saying that something is socially constructed (rather than natural or biological) doesn't mean that it doesn't feel real to us. Or that it's easy to change. We internalize social messages on such a deep level that they become engraved in our psyches. What initially enters our constitution from the outside world comes to function as an ingrained (seemingly inherent) component of our identity. After a while, we take socially constructed meanings to be indisputable facts; we forget that such meanings are not timeless truths but rather reflect collective values that have evolved over centuries of human efforts to understand the world.

Gender stereotypes are among the most tenacious of such cultural fictions. There's simply no way to disentangle them from biology, or even from the ways in which biologists choose to study biology. When it comes to Fisher's evolutionary explanations, the line between biology and culture gets so blurry as to make some of her observations completely untenable.

In the context of describing male and female courting rituals, Fisher offers this pearl of wisdom: "If the man is courting, he pays—and a woman almost instinctively knows her partner is wooing her." *Instinctively?* A woman's understanding that there's a correlation between a guy paying for dinner and romantic intent is *instinctive?* It has nothing to do with the fact that every romantic comedy she's ever seen, every steamy Harlequin novel she's ever read, every *Cosmo* article she's ever devoured has told her—along with her frail grandmother and her nosy aunt—that a man's got to pay for dinner if he's going to get into her knickers?

But wait, it gets better. Fisher speculates that women don't like sports because their female ancestors left hunting to the males: "What is a football game but a map, a maze, a puzzle, spatial action, and aggressive competition—all of which engage skills that appeal to the male brain. In fact, watching a football game on television is not very different from sitting behind a bush on the African veldt, trying to judge which route the giraffes will take. No wonder most women do not understand why men get such pleasure from watching sports; these pastimes don't ring a chord in their evolutionary psyches."

You've got to be kidding me. The hapless giraffes on the African veldt are to blame for the Super Bowl? But hold on! What about the fact that every time I go to Fenway Park for the Red Sox, it's packed with women? Are they all there for Adrián Béltre's taut butt? And why is my mother glued to the television screen whenever the Olympics are on? Or the World Cup? Or the U.S.-Canada hockey game? Even when *The Bold and the Beautiful* is summoning from a competing channel, she would rather watch a bunch of sweaty guys chase a hockey puck.

My friend Patrick has the same problem with his wife, Trish (a nurse). Apparently, she watches sports so much that he's rarely able to catch CNN. And then there are all those women who actually *play* sports. Basketball. Soccer. Lacrosse. Hockey. Not to mention all those track-and-field athletes, skiers, skaters, swimmers, marathon runners, and rock climbers. Did they all miss some major evolutionary step? Don't they know that sports shouldn't "ring a chord" in their spatially challenged psyches? And, for God's sake, when is Serena Williams going to admit that the design of the tennis court is too complicated for her female brain?

4

If I belabor the obvious, it's because I'm baffled that "science" such as this gets through the censors when there's overwhelming evidence that it's blatantly inaccurate. When it comes to romance, Fisher herself admits that we form highly specific "love maps" by the time we're eight. These maps come into being in response to our families, friends, educators, and other environmental influences. Far from being biologically determined, they arise from social interactions that teach us to appreciate some human traits and temperaments more than others. Over time, they solidify into an unconscious mental picture of "your perfect mate, the settings you find enticing, and the kinds of conversations and erotic activities that excite you." When you fall in love with a man, you project this map onto him. You find in him some of the qualities that you have learned to desire. But if this is the case, why bother with all the talk about biology?

When outlining patterns of attraction, Fisher claims that while standards of beauty and sex appeal vary wildly from society to society, there are some universals. Because of the ever-present evolutionary imperative to produce babies, men are attracted to women who are likely to give birth to viable offspring. So they choose young women with shiny teeth, skin, eyes, and hair. Women, in turn, go for good providers: Men with money, power, property, and prestige. In addition, because of something called "positive assortive mating," we tend to marry people like ourselves in terms of ethnicity and education.

All of this is *biological*, of course. I entered the world knowing that I should aim for the Ivy-League grad with a high IQ and witty tongue. My attraction to this guy has nothing to do with the fact that I spent fifteen years interacting with exactly these kinds of men. Or that I'm still surrounded by them on a daily basis. Fisher would have me believe that I'm more likely to date an overachieving, slightly neurotic Ivy-League grad than a "gentle, poetic carpenter" because of some evolutionary imprint I carry from time immemorial. Personally, I think it might have something to do with the fact that I've only met one poetic carpenter in my life. Tragically, he was already taken. In contrast, the overachieving, slightly neurotic Ivy-League types are pretty hard for me to avoid. I meet a few dozen every time I go to an academic conference. And it's impossible to walk the short distance from the front door of my office building to my office without coming across at least a couple of these pesky types.

Let's admit that wealth and prestige can be attractive. And that shiny eyes and skin can be a turn-on. But let's not pretend that men can't appreciate a woman with money.

Or that women can't appreciate a man with shiny hair. The minute women have as much money and power in our society as (some) men do, they might well prefer the struggling singer over the Wall Street shark. An alarming percentage of us already do. Particularly if the guy has shiny (but disheveled) hair. And as soon as our culture stops worshipping youth and beauty (unlikely, but one can always dream), men might start choosing older, slightly less shiny women. Even now, some guys are dumb enough to date women who are past their child-bearing years. Someone should pull them aside and tell them that they're bringing evolutionary progress to a screeching halt.

No doubt, there are gendered patterns in our society. Men frequent strip clubs more often than women. And women are more likely to coo at babies in public (what men do in the privacy of their own homes is another matter). But such differences do not necessarily have a biological base. Human beings have intricate systems of culture, ethics, politics, and linguistic capacity. We have consciousness. Even more importantly, we have an unconscious that carries a record of our past experiences. We might even have souls. Science that overlooks all of this is, quite simply, bad science.

Yet many people in our society are seduced by "science" such as this. This is because it confirms what they already believe (what they are culturally conditioned to believe). They are receptive to evolutionary models because such models seem to give a solid foundation for our cultural organization. They bring stability to our lives by reassuring us that the way things are is how they are meant to be.

Think of the cultural chaos that would ensue if desperate housewives everywhere started to go to strip clubs in throngs. Or if Wall Street types in Brooks Brothers suits stopped baby carriages on the sidewalk to coo at cute babies. Biological models are comforting because they tell us that these kinds of things won't happen. They simplify our lives by giving them an appearance of order. But this order exacts an enormous price. It places restrictions on us that flatten the human complexity of all of us. These restrictions confine men almost as much as women. They send men the message that they have to suppress the more emotional, more sensitive side of themselves to count as men. They tell men that there's something wrong with them if they aren't excited over every pair of boobs that passes them on the street. As a result, loosening our stereotypical notions of what men and women are (naturally) like would be as liberating to men as it would to women. It would open up a whole new array of human possibilities for both genders.

5

Collective stereotypes about men and women are a social pathology that traps us in narrow-minded notions about how relationships are supposed to work. They keep us imprisoned in predictable romantic routines. Worst of all, they divide men and women into opposing "camps." This almost automatically implies that one side is better than the other. And it suggests that the relationship between them is inherently antagonistic—that in order for me to "win," my guy must somehow "lose." In addition, supposedly only a massive interpretive effort can bridge the differences between us. We are fated to misunderstand each others' motives for the rest of our lives. This may be. But is this really a matter of gender? If two women date each other, will they be completely transparent to each other just because they're both women? Will they automatically sidestep any and all relationship problems? I doubt it.

I resist categorical pronouncements about men and women because I suspect that they keep us from appreciating the finer gradations of love. They cause us to resort to hackneyed relationship strategies at those very moments when a more flexible approach might lead to a better outcome. They prevent us from recognizing the human integrity of those we love, for the more we box men and women into rigid categories, the less we are able to cherish each individual, each lover, for who he or she actually is.

I'm not saying that men and women are the same. I'm saying that each individual is unique. When a specific man and a specific woman fall in love with each other, the complex reality of their relationship far surpasses stereotypical notions of what men and women are supposed to be like. Undoubtedly, some people are attracted to partners who approximate such stereotypes. But others are attracted to those who challenge them. And the latter are a growing segment of the population because more and more of us recognize that stereotypes prevent us from having the kinds of multifaceted relationships we want. We understand that the more stereotypical our ways of relating, the less alive we feel both as individuals and lovers. What could be more boring than a guy who thinks that emotions undermine his manliness? Or who is threatened by my ability to set up the DVD player? Or who never lets me drive his stick-shift (literally or figuratively)? And don't even try to sell me a guy who thinks that baseball is too complicated for girls!

There's one huge advantage to recognizing that gender is a social construct rather than a biological necessity: We can change how we live our gendered lives. Not easily. As I've explained, social constructs are obstinate. They're almost as difficult to shift as biological necessities. But they still give us more leeway. If we believe that men and women are naturally different, there's nothing we can do to modify things. But if we believe that a large part of masculinity and femininity is culturally conditioned, we can begin to work toward a place of mutual understanding. We can fashion more democratic gender systems where both men and women are free to express all sides of their being. And we can build new models for romance—models that allow us to love more creatively, more passionately.

I like chimps as much as the next person. But they're not where I would go for ideas on how to love better. If a chimp society ever produces a Galileo, an Einstein, a Marie Curie, or even a working elevator, I might be willing to sit down for a chat. But until then, I'm going to assume that they don't know anything that we don't already know.

The changes that have taken place in human society during the last hundred years alone are mind-boggling. From Virginia Woolf to Picasso, Elvis, Louis Armstrong, Rosa Parks, man on the moon, birth control, Indira Gandhi, Akira Kurosawa, the fall of the Berlin Wall, Advil, Madonna, the Internet, heart surgery, and President Obama to BlackBerries and smartphones, humans have cleared one hurdle after another. There's nothing that compares to this in chimp societies. Or in any other animal societies. What separates humans from other animals is the incredible speed of our progress (as well as our incredible capacity for destruction). Frankly, it shocks me that a society that has managed to produce test-tube babies, *Avatar*, skyscrapers, sunblock, and some of the best Italian food in the world is looking to chimps for prototypes of romantic behavior.

Why are we trying to explain the current realities of romance by some evolutionary past? Why not transcend it instead? Isn't that what humans do? Aren't we driven to exceed whatever has become outdated? The leap from being able to rub two sticks together to produce fire (something that chimps, by the way, have yet to master) to my central heating system is not negligible. Nor is the distance between chimp language and Wordsworth, Emily Dickinson, T. S. Eliot, Maya Angelou, and Pablo Neruda. Why, then, insist that the gap between animal reproductive instinct and human romantic arrangements is virtually nonexistent? Or, worse still, that the future of human relationships should reflect some pre-historic past that we no longer have access to? While we're

at it, why not insist that we go back to eating raw meat, picking ticks out of each others' hair, and shamelessly scratching
ourselves in front of our neighbors?

Why is romance singled out as the *one* domain of human
life where the less evolved we are, the better off we're somehow supposed to be? Why, in short, scour animal societies
for romantic ideals? Why not turn to human imagination
instead? This imagination has never been constrained by
biology. It has never shown humility in the face of tradition.
Why start now? Why hold back love when the rest of society
leaps forward?

CHAPTER 4

········

For Better Romantic Advice, Watch *Gossip Girl*

MYTH: Television shows offer mindless entertainment that fries our brains.

FACT: Some of the most advanced thinking about men, women, and romance takes place on television.

1

I'm not joking. If I had a choice between the evolutionary biological model of romance and Nate Archibald, I would pick Nate every day of the week. If you don't know who Nate is, do me a favor and watch an episode of *Gossip Girl*. It won't take you long to spot him. He's the one with shiny teeth, skin, eyes, and hair. So shiny! Helen Fisher would have me believe that these are "feminine" traits that shouldn't matter to me— that I should be attracted to his wealth and status instead. Wrong. Very wrong. There are times when I can't decide if I would rather have Nate or be Nate. I want to know which shampoo he uses.

And guess what? What really attracts me about this guy is that he's not a knuckle-dragging Neanderthal. He's not your average macho aggressor. And neither are the other guys of the show. Chuck Bass tries his best, but even he can't pull it off. His colorful neckties and lapel arrangements land him closer to Oscar Wilde than a caveman. It's hard to pin any of the *Gossip Girl* guys on an evolutionary map that leads from chimps to men. *Ain't that a relief?* Those who are looking for some ape-loving are welcome to stick to *Two and a Half Men*. Me? I would rather pull the petals off a daisy to decide which one of the *Gossip Girl* hotties I would most like to...er...invite for a cup of coffee. Nate. Chuck. Dan. Nate. Chuck. Dan.

When it comes to gender, *Gossip Girl* gives me hope. Sure, the plotlines are ridiculous. And yes, the show transmits impossible ideals of beauty. The actors are so gorgeous that it's hard not to develop an inferiority complex. Yet those responsible for writing the show—and others like it—have figured out something that many relationship "experts" have not, namely that the most desirable men and women these days are those who shatter gender stereotypes rather than fortify them.

This is most obvious in shows aimed at young audiences. When you think of recent teen hit shows such as *Gossip Girl, Gilmore Girls, The O.C., Glee, 90210, One Tree Hill,* or *Smallville*, it's clear that they capitalize on the incredible charisma of characters who do not conform to traditional notions of what it means to be an attractive man or woman. These shows are chock-full of strong, smart, ambitious, confident, and competent female characters. And—what's maybe even more striking—their leading men are usually a far cry from the emotionally unavailable men of self-help guides. If anything, we are served a steady diet of tender, thoughtful, and broken-hearted guys whose yearning for love matches that of Madame Bovary.

And these guys know how to communicate! From *The O.C.*'s Seth Cohen to *One Tree Hill*'s Lucas Scott, these young men know how to talk about their feelings. Whole episodes are made of these feelings. They talk about the meaning of life, the meaning of love, the meaning of loss, and the meaning of having to let go. They even talk about books and poetry. They talk to other guys. They talk to their dads. And they definitely talk to women—from moms to sisters to friends to girlfriends. One of the main messages of these shows is that the worst thing a guy could do would be to keep his feelings inside. Whenever he does, some disaster ensues. He ends up in a bar fight. He loses his family fortune. His best friend gets in a car accident. His girlfriend leaves him. Or someone dies. So we learn from episode to episode, season to season, that good communication is the key to the good life—that the man-in-his-cave model really doesn't work. And before you start telling me that this is all make-believe—that guys in the real world don't function this way—let me assure you that most guys I know are regular chatterboxes. At least those under forty. I find that most younger men will tell you their deepest, darkest secrets if you give them half a chance. And they're not energy vampires, either. No matter how caught up they get in their tale, at some point they'll turn things around with a generous "And what about you?" They're nice that way. Real nice.

Don't get me wrong. The shows I'm talking about contain their obligatory allotment of ditzy blondes, scheming bitches, hopeless klutzes, insensitive jocks, and pathetic nerds. They are racially homogenous to a disturbing degree, with core casts of well-scrubbed white folks. And some of their main characters—such as *The O.C.*'s Ryan and Marissa (the show's very own James Dean and Marilyn Monroe)—recycle predictable gender tropes that echo the ideals of times long past. But more often than not, much of the allure of the main characters arises from their refusal to uphold conventional gender roles. The romantic anguish of the three heartthrobs of *Gossip Girl* drives the show as much as the diabolic designs of Blair Waldorf or even the sex appeal of Serena van der Woodsen. *One Tree Hill* offers us the sensitive writer-want-to-be Lucas. *90210* the ever-attentive Navid. *Glee* the football-hunk-with-a-heart-of-gold Finn. *The O.C.* the nerdy-yet-adorable Seth (you'll know that the times truly have changed when you realize that the scrawny Adam Brody is a sex symbol with the power to make teen girls scream). And the popular rewrite of the Superman saga, *Smallville*, hands us a psychologically intense, heart-wrenchingly tortured, chronically lovelorn, and hopelessly conflicted Clark Kent. Today's Prince Charming is as likely to charm us with his emotional woundability as with his rugged masculinity.

Take Chuck, *Gossip Girl*'s self-proclaimed womanizer. Chuck's bad-boy appeal is undeniable. Yet it's less *Rocky*-ish than metrosexual. We're dealing with a twenty-first century dandy rather than with a standard specimen of manly magnetism. And what ultimately wins us over is the subtle play of suffering on Chuck's face in the aftermath of one of Blair's frequent snubs. We relate to this character because, underneath the bravado, there's a self-doubting heart that longs for love and acceptance as much as the rest of us. Likewise, while there's pleasure to be had in watching Clark Kent super-speed from Smallville to Metropolis in a blink of an eye, blast his way into Lex Luthor's safe (why does this safe always contain green kryptonite?), and fold the (always conveniently unconscious) Lois Lane into his protective arms, Tom Welling's Clark is at his most compelling when he reveals his weaknesses—when his shyness or romantic uncertainty keep him from getting the girl.

2

I don't think that it's accidental that the most frequent romantic attitude displayed by the male characters of these shows is one of hesitancy and touching vulnerability. If these shows activate a female fantasy about masculinity at its most delectable—which they obviously do—it's notable that this fantasy has much more to do with characteristics that women might share with men than with emblematic markers of manliness.

It of course helps to look like Tom Welling, Chase Crawford, Ed Westwick, or Chad Michael Murray. These actors get away with gender-bending in part because no one in her right mind would question their desirability. Still,

I would argue that their characters tell us a lot about contemporary romantic ideals. They prove that the "rules" of romance—if there ever was such a thing—are no longer the same as they might have been twenty years ago. And I don't think that women's wishful thinking alone accounts for the change, for young men as well as women watch these shows. There is something about the insecurities of the male characters that speaks to young men of our time.

What does it mean that male and female audiences alike fawn over *Glee*'s Finn—a guy who is as good at singing a love ballad as he is at scoring a goal? And what do we make of the fact that it's the artsy Rufus Humphrey—*Gossip Girl*'s emotionally savvy dad who also cooks a mean breakfast—rather than the tough businessman (and Chuck's cold father), Bart Bass, who has come to stand for the modern teenager's ideal dad?

There's a key scene in Episode 12 of Season 3 of *Gossip Girl* that more or less sums up the show's take on masculinity. It's the first anniversary of Bart's death. Chuck is struggling to come to terms with his realization that he hasn't turned out to be the man that his father wanted him to be. Even though Chuck is an accomplished businessman, he can't bring himself to be as ruthless as his father was. As the day advances, Chuck keeps having visions of his father who derides him for not being able to force a group of homeless people out of a building he wants to convert into upscale lofts. Bart tells Chuck that opening his heart to Blair has made him weak and soft—that he can't expect to be an effective businessman as long as he also insists on being a loving boyfriend.

The culmination of the episode comes when Chuck (for reasons that would take us too far off-track) is forced to revisit the hospital where his father died. When Blair finds him in one of the corridors, crouched on the floor and shaking, they have the following exchange:

> Chuck: My father always thought I was weak. And in the moment that it mattered most, I was. I couldn't be there when he died. I left right away. I've been pushing myself to prove him wrong. And...I'm pushing you away.

> Blair: I don't think you ran away because you couldn't handle death. I think it's because you couldn't handle feelings. But you're not like that any more. You're strong. You carry people. You carry me. You're becoming a man in a way that your father never was.

The message couldn't be clearer. Bart is right that Chuck has changed. He's no longer the unfeeling playboy he used to be. But this is what makes him strong. The fact that he now knows how to handle feelings makes him a man with more dimension than his father ever had. Blair's comment draws an equation between manhood, feelings, and strength. This equation is what modern masculinity is made out of. This masculinity "carries" others much more effectively than Sherry Argov's bug-killing Tarzan. Fortunately for women, the Bart Basses of the world are increasingly a relic of the past. They might deserve a display case somewhere near the dinosaurs in the Washington Museum of Natural History. But, as the male leads of *Gossip Girl* and other television shows confirm, they're no longer a suitable role model for the young men of today.

And the female leads? There's no doubt that they do their fair share of pining. And they mend their crushed hearts with Godiva truffles with predictable regularity. But they're usually also sassy, talented, intelligent, highly motivated, and sometimes even blatantly competitive. They want to excel. They go after their goals even at the expense of their romantic success. And, thankfully, their friends never let them wallow in their post-breakup misery beyond the point where a broken heart might turn into a broken spirit.

What's fascinating about female characters such as Rory of *Gilmore Girls*, Vanessa of *Gossip Girl*, Rachel of *Glee*, Silver of *90210*, and Lois of *Smallville* is that they manage to be beguiling not despite, but because of, their intellect and ambition. Sure, if solving a murder takes a bit of pole-dancing at a local gentlemen's club, Erica Durance's curvaceous body will take you further than your IQ. But if those curves did not come with Lois's feisty and independent attitude, we wouldn't like her nearly as much. And neither would most modern guys. The Playboy bunny can't hold a candle to Lois's combination of self-assured sensuality, physical hardiness, mental sharpness, prickly banter, and obstinate self-sufficiency. Lois Lane was always a tough girl. Now she's even more so. Her kung fu moves would make Wesley Snipes proud.

Hollywood has long recognized the allure of a sexy woman

who is also tough as nails. From Angelina Jolie's *Tomb Raider* and Jennifer Garner's *Alias* to the female characters of shows such as *24*, *CSI*, *Law and Order*, *Missing*, *The Closer*, *Bones*, and *Criminal Minds*, the entertainment industry is banking on the combination of beauty and brawn to create gripping female leads. A cynic might say that there's nothing that sells more than a gun-toting, half-naked action heroine who barely breaks a sweat in defeating a bunch of baddies. Such a cynic would be right, of course. Yet something more promising is also going on. We are witnessing a drastic renegotiation of the cultural coordinates of femininity and masculinity.

Take *Bones*. The title character, Temperance "Bones" Brennan, is a brilliant and hyper-motivated scientist whose main flaw is her social awkwardness and inability to read the emotional cues of others. She and her best friend, Angela, both have voracious sex drives. And they both suffer from commitment jitters whenever a lover gets too close. In contrast, Brennan's FBI partner, Booth, is a warm and compassionate guy with plenty of emotional intelligence—a committed (single) dad and accomplished interpreter of feelings. The show's success hinges primarily on its skillful reversal of traditional gender expectations.

3

Interestingly, many of the shows I've alluded to acknowledge that they go against the grain of gender expectations by making some of their characters struggle with the implications of not fitting into cultural ideals. *Glee*'s Rachel, for instance, knows that her ambition may scare off guys. The show consistently pits her against the conventionally pretty cheerleader, Quinn, to highlight the price of not conforming. The show's Finn, in turn, has to come to terms with the loss of social standing that results from his "wimpy" decision to join a glee club. Along similar lines, *Smallville*'s Chloe Sullivan—one of the smartest women on television—repeatedly finds herself romantically overshadowed by the more luscious Lois. Yet, ironically, viewers know that Chloe is not a suitable partner for Clark because she's ultimately not tough enough. We know that Lois will succeed where Chloe fails because Lois's unapologetically brassy attitude makes her a fitting match for a superhero.

Some shows place the challenge of navigating a minefield of revised gender roles at their very heart. An early example of this was the 1990s teen show *Dawson's Creek*, where Katie Holmes's brainy tomboy character spent several seasons agonizing over not being girly enough. A more recent example is *Lipstick Jungle*, a series based on a novel by Candace Bushnell (the author of *Sex and the City*). The series—pitched at a slightly older audience than the shows I've been talking about—details the lives and loves of three high-powered women in New York. In the pilot episode, Wendy (a movie executive played by Brooke Shields) discovers that her husband can't quite cope with having a wife who is more successful than he is. Nico (an editor-in-chief played by Kim Raver), in turn, finds out that her boss is hesitant to promote her to a position for which she's highly qualified because he believes that men and women are "wired" differently, and that women, consequently, aren't cut out for the competitive world of publishing.

Within the first twenty minutes of the show, we see the complications that John Gray's Mars-Venus model can cause for professional women who are constantly asked to prove that they are not Venus—that they're not "wired" like girls. We see how easily the notion of different "wiring" becomes an excuse to keep women out of the higher echelons of the work force. It in fact puts women in an impossible bind. The ones who admit to being Venus get weeded out because they're supposedly not tough enough. And the ones who deny being Venus—the ones who put up a fight to show that they are tough enough—get weeded out because...well, because they're not real women; they're freaks of nature.

Debra Messing's series, *The Starter Wife*, foregrounds similar concerns. The show sketches the hilarious (yet also poignant) efforts of Molly, a forty-something ex-wife of a Hollywood producer, to pull her life together after her husband suddenly leaves her for a younger woman. In the first few episodes, we find Molly in emotional disarray, (literally) coming undone at the seams when she starts eating normally after the twelve-year "diet" that was also her marriage. We learn that when she got married, Molly gave up a promising writing career to foster her husband's ambitions. Her entire life, up until the divorce, revolved around her untiring efforts to be the perfect Hollywood wife, to run an immaculate household, to look the part at parties, and to cater to her husband's every personal and professional whim. She was as good at finding her husband's socks as she was at entertaining his high-powered guests. Her life had meaning as long as he was content.

The divorce shatters Molly's world. What follows are her painstaking exertions to rebuild her life and to discover her potential as an individual and a professional woman. We get to watch her gradual rise from the ashes as her writing career takes off. We witness her miraculous transformation from a social pariah to a self-possessed author courted by high-society divas and hunky lovers alike. And we are delighted to learn that the more successful and assertive Molly becomes, the better her love life gets. Her accomplishments make her so attractive that even her egotistical ex-husband comes around for a romantic retake. He doesn't stand a chance with the reformed Molly, though. She's way beyond him. She's way beyond anything she herself could have imagined prior to the divorce.

The plot of *The Starter Wife* couldn't be more predictable. What could be a bigger platitude than the story of a spurned woman who heroically fights her way from the pits of self-pity and humiliation to career glory and romantic victory (while also managing to stay enviably slim without ever dieting again)? Throw in an alcoholic best friend, an over-the-top gay guy, a couple of gifted black supporting actors, and a mysterious love interest, and you have the Hollywood run-of-the-mill formula for a romantic comedy. Besides good writing, Messing's considerable comedic appeal, and the undeniable talent of the supporting cast, what keeps the series from spiraling into banalities is its capacity to ruthlessly mock its own clichés. But what's maybe even more important is its ability to touch a collective cultural nerve about gender and romance.

Molly's explicit investment in the question of what it means to be a modern woman with both professional and romantic aspirations speaks to women who are caught up in sweeping cultural shifts that can be confusing for everyone involved (including the men in our lives). It's significant that the first season of the show ends with Molly breaking up with her sexy novelist boyfriend, Zach. She tells him that she has come to realize that the relationship will never work because what he wants is the "old Molly"—the Molly who would have been willing to shelve her ambitions for the sake of a man. The new Molly—the multilayered woman she has become—is no longer able to do so. The disconnect between their romantic expectations ends the relationship. He's too old-school for her. She wants a guy who will respect her career as much as she respects his. Viewers realize that she'll end up getting this. Eventually. We understand that she'll end the series snuggled up with a guy just like this. The fact that the parting shot of Zach shows him miserable and questioning his out-of-date values implies that it could even be him. But I suspect Molly can do better.

Not bad for prime-time television. Not bad at all. The moral of the story is that those who are unwilling to adjust to the more fluid gender dynamic of our time will lose out.

They may not "fail" in love per se. They may end up in nominally "successful" relationships and marriages. And they may even have an easier time at it because the old "rules" are less bewildering than the new reality. But the implication is that they will squander their chances at genuinely fulfilling relationships. They will never reap the benefits of an equal partnership where both parties are encouraged to evolve into self-realized individuals who are not afraid to pursue their own goals even as they build a common future.

4

What's equally noteworthy is that these shows urge us to love with unadulterated passion. They give us permission to take romantic risks. I'm not naïve. I know television and movie fantasies are unrealistic. Their ardor is beyond the reach of ordinary mortals. We're presented with highly idealized men and women whose emotional states, personal struggles, relationship dilemmas, and romantic disappointments are intensified for the sake of dramatic impact. This is something that students in my pop culture classes often comment on. Those who watch a lot of television report that they sometimes end up acting in ways that reflect the fantasy landscapes of their favorite shows. Their sense of identification is so strong that they start to copy speech patterns and emotional lexicons. When their boyfriend says something insensitive, they throw a hysterical fit like Naomi from 90210. Or they resort to some theatrical gesture they picked up from Glee. This can be a problem. But there's something to be said for the fact that these shows encourage women to speak their mind. And there's also something to be said for their capacity to rouse our snoozing passions. If we're riveted, it's because these shows speak to our longing for larger-than-life romance. They speak to our yearning for something that we're in danger of losing in real life.

Our self-help culture promotes the idea that love should be safe. It tries to give love a clear plotline and a clear destination: Take the right twelve steps in the right sequence and marriage will follow. Anything with even a hint of ambiguity is discouraged. If you think you might get hurt, back away. If you suspect danger, retract your investment. Better safe than sorry. Don't fall so hard that you can't easily recover. The worst you could do would be to lose control. The less you let yourself be swept into passion's deceptive cloud, the bigger your share of the love pie will eventually be. And don't under any circumstances give more than you get. Stay a little stingy. Make your guy prove himself to you. Test his love. And then test it again. Even when you're pretty sure it's trustworthy, make him jump a few more hurdles. Just in case. You can never be too careful. Or too calculating. It's your heart we're talking about, after all!

This mentality pathologizes those who jump before they look. It makes us worry that being bold (and generous) with our affections might mean that there's something amiss with us. Television shows pull us in the opposite direction. All the passion that we can't allow ourselves to experience in real life is channeled into these screen fantasies. Undoubtedly, this is a little disconcerting. There's something troubling about the fact that, instead of living passion, we get our pleasure from watching fictional characters enact it for us. But at least these screen fantasies keep alive the idea that love is linked to chaotic and unmanageable sentiments. And they also stress that when we get hurt in love, it's often not anyone's fault. It's not because our partner plotted to wound us, or because we did something wrong. It's because love is, by its nature, muddled and unpredictable. And it's because people lead complex lives where other things can get in the way of love. Sometimes you've got to go save the world before you can cuddle on the couch with your honey (Clark Kent's dilemma). Sometimes you really are too hung up on a girl to move on (Seth Cohen's dilemma). And sometimes the person you most want is the one you can't allow yourself to have (Chuck Bass's dilemma).

Television shows highlight the ambivalence of love. Their intricate web of desire and deception reveals that emotions are rarely simple. That there are times when people don't take action when they should, and others when they act prematurely. Sometimes you end up with the wrong person. Other times you end up with the right person at the wrong time. Sometimes you get a second chance. Sometimes you get no chance at all. There are times when it's all about unrequited yearning, and others when you get your happy ending. But the one thing that doesn't happen on television is that you sit down with your best friend to discuss ways to safety-check romance. No, on television, you don't expect love to be reliable. You're willing to stake your heart. If you're Blair Waldorf, you chase the bad boy. And if you're Lois Lane, you definitely don't shy away from mysterious men. You fall for every super-hero in town even though they keep disappearing on you in the middle of a make-out session. They're always running off to rescue someone from an armed robbery or a train accident. You don't know this, so you're a little hurt when they rush off without an explanation. But you don't make the mistake of thinking that this is because you've somehow blown your game. You may give the guy a hard time later. Or you may get so annoyed that you dump him. But you don't scold yourself for having been too available, or for not having enough self-esteem. If you're Lois Lane, you have self-esteem. And you know that the blunders of love are an inescapable part of life.

5

The guys are equally willing to wager their hearts. One of the many things I like about the *Gossip Girl* men is that they love with an almost desperate dedication. They may have a string of affairs along the way just to keep the plot moving. But when they really love, it's with the same kind of fixation as the female characters do.

In the very first episode, we have Nate refusing to have sex with his (then) girlfriend, Blair, because he's secretly in love with Serena. In Season 2, Chuck runs into performance problems with his hired companions because he can't get Blair out of his mind. And, in Season 3, Dan flees from the bed of an attractive Tisch student because he has just realized that he's in love with Vanessa. All of this is worth paying attention to because so much of our culture—including our self-help culture—tells us that men are always ready for sex. That a red-blooded guy is looking to bed any reasonably attractive woman who crosses his path. Supposedly, who that woman is as a person doesn't matter, as long as she possesses the right body parts.

I've got to say that I'm with *Gossip Girl* on this one. I find that when my male friends are lusting after a particular woman (which is often), or trying to get over a breakup (which is equally often), they're not in the least bit interested in other women. It's just as difficult for them to transfer their desire to a new object as it is for many women. If they're truly smitten, it doesn't matter how many sex kittens you put in front of them. They would rather reach for that gallon of Breyers—or that bottle of Jack Daniel's—than betray their love. And all along they'll be obsessively checking their email, voice mail, text mail, snail mail, and all other possible forms of mail. When they get completely dejected, they'll even scan the horizon for carrier pigeons.

At a key moment in Season 3 of *Gossip Girl*, Dan sums up the modern guy's "choice" as follows: Utter emotional vulnerability with a woman he loves or meaningless sex with a total stranger. There may be men in the world who repeatedly opt for the latter. Some of these are the traditional macho type. But others are guys who are terrified of getting burned. Dan is also terrified, but (because television guys are emotionally brave), he chooses love. As does Nate. In the middle of the same season, Nate confesses to Serena that he has been in love with her for more than three years. What's even better, when they finally get into a relationship, they discover that self-help games get them absolutely nowhere. Serena's attempt to make Nate jealous backfires. And Nate's resolution to hide the immensity of his feelings alienates Serena. It's one terrible misunderstanding after another. Until they decide to drop the game. That's when they end up making out in the coat-check room of a French ambassador's mansion.

How could I not love this show?

Modern men know how to long for a woman. In fact, men throughout the ages have been good at the fine art of pining. When you think of the most famous male lovers in history, it's immediately obvious that many of them were hopeless romantics. Whether you're talking about Tristan and Iseult, Dante and Beatrice, Romeo and Juliet, or Werther and Lotte, you can't avoid noticing that you're dealing with men who will do anything for the woman they love (including killing themselves—not something I endorse). There's no question of sleeping around.

It's only recently—during the twentieth century?—that we've come to believe that longing is "feminine" and running after easy sex is "masculine." What I like about contemporary television shows is that they swing the pendulum back. They show that men ache for love as much as women do. And if you're Tom Welling's Superman, you ache more than a mere mortal could ever bear. You kiss Lana Lang (Superman's pre-Lois girlfriend) even when she has been infected by kryptonite so that getting close to her sends green shoots of agony through your entire system.

It would be easy to ridicule this kind of intensity. But if the message is that men are emotionally fragile creatures just like women are, I am inclined to welcome it. I'm also inclined to welcome the idea that it's okay to love fervently—with a legendary and single-minded devotion. It's okay to throw yourself in first and think second. In our overly cautious self-help culture, television shows that highlight plotlines of immense love and immense loss are doing us a favor. To be sure, on some level they feed our sappy Hallmark sensibilities. But they also remind us that, as a romantic culture, we need to feel more rather than less. If we're drawn to these shows, it's because, deep down, we sense that something is missing from our lives. We long for something bigger. We yearn for what is awe-inspiring and spirit-awakening.

Each period in history has had its mythologies—its heroic tales of great trials and ever greater triumphs. The Greeks had *The Iliad* and *The Odyssey*. The Middle Ages had Dante. The Renaissance had Shakespearean tragedies. The Romantics had Goethe and Byron. Victorian England had Charlotte Brontë. We have *Gossip Girl*. This may seem deplorable. But in the absence of a convincing contender, I wouldn't want to underestimate the show's power to keep alive sentiments that have few other places to go in our culture. I wouldn't want to scoff at the cosmic proportions of the passions that the show—and others like it—puts in front of us on a weekly basis.

CHAPTER 5

....

Modern Cinderellas Look beyond the Prince's Ball

> **MYTH:** The best way to win a man's heart is to play into his fantasies of feminine desirability.
>
> **FACT:** This is one of the best ways to get your heart broken.

1

For all my urgency about the need to rescue love from the idea that it should be safe, there are some romantic scenarios I would strongly caution you against. More specifically, it's important to avoid relationships that hurt not only when they end but also while they last. There's a big difference between taking a romantic risk on the one hand and resigning yourself to long-term misery on the other. While there is no way to protect yourself from love's painful endings, it's essential to avoid bad romances that *won't* end.

If a guy slaps you around, screams at you, humiliates you, or puts you down on a regular basis, I trust you'll know that you're in an abusive relationship. However, there are forms of abuse that sneak up on you so subtly that it can take a long time to recognize that something is wrong. Among these is one particularly perilous trap: Narcissistic and self-absorbed men. These guys can pulverize your self-esteem faster than it takes your average coffee grinder to produce enough grounds for two cups of coffee. They will insist that each and every relationship crisis is due to some personal shortcoming of yours. By the time you begin to realize that you're not the problem, you might be so deep in the mess that you can't get out without losing a major chunk of your confidence. This is why it's crucial to look beyond the prince's ball whenever you catch yourself stepping into Cinderella's dainty shoes.

I know no better allegory for narcissistic love than a famous short story called "The Sandman." This tale of obsession and intrigue was written by the nineteenth-century German writer E. T. A. Hoffmann. In it, a young man named Nathanael abandons his down-to-earth fiancée, Clara, for an enigmatic beauty, Olympia. During much of the story, Olympia sits motionless in her bedroom as Nathanael spies on her from his room in a neighboring building (if you sense echoes of Hitchcock here, you'll shortly see that you're on the right track). Olympia's other accomplishments include playing the piano and dancing with perfunctory precision. And she responds to Nathanael's every statement with a gentle "Ah, ah!" The reader's mounting unease is resolved when we learn that Olympia is a doll fabricated by Nathanael's physics professor, Spalanzani, and a sinister lens maker, Coppola. Her sparkling eyes are made of glass. Her measured movements are controlled by a clockwork mechanism embedded in her

slender body. And "Ah, ah!" are the only words she is programmed to utter. Toward the end of the story, she's destroyed
when Spalanzani and Coppola fight over her inert body.

Hoffmann's story highlights the structure of narcissistic
love. It contrasts the spirited Clara with the bland beauty of
Olympia to show that what Nathanael worships in Olympia
is a reflection of himself. Olympia's pretty eyes mirror
back to Nathanael an image of himself that he likes. And
her pliant "Ah, ah!" confirms the wisdom of everything he
says. Nathanael pours the depths of his soul to Olympia.
And the more she affirms him, the more validated he feels.
What Nathanael doesn't see is that Olympia is able to echo
the movements of his soul only because she herself doesn't
have one. And she replicates Nathanael's thoughts because
she is incapable of formulating her own. Nathanael chooses
Olympia over Clara because Olympia's lack of personality
makes her an ideal screen for his egotistical projections. She
is the perfect woman, the ultimate fantasy object.

2

There are, unfortunately, men in the world who are a lot like
Nathanael. I once knew a guy, Ethan, who walked around with
a mental list of ideal qualities he looked for in a woman. In
part, this reflected his pragmatic approach to life in general.
He liked to plan every detail of his future. And he wanted to
make sure that his romantic destiny would unfurl as logically
as the rest of his life. But, ultimately, his "list" was motivated

by a narcissistic wish to find a woman who would confirm the high opinion he already held of himself.

As a man of considerable wealth and social status, Ethan calculated that he had the right to expect his partner to fulfill certain standards of desirability. Believing in a "market-value" theory of relationships, he thought that any woman worthy of his attention would need to bring some tangible "assets" to the table. His measurement kit consisted of four main criteria: looks, wealth, intellect, and social refinement. If a woman fell short in one of these categories, she needed to make up for it in one of the others. On top of all of this, he had a wish list of physical attributes, detailing body type, height, hair color, age range, ability to bear children, and such.

Not surprisingly, Ethan alienated one girlfriend after another. He found a way to justify each separation by recourse to some flaw in the woman who walked out on him, so that she was "needy," "fragile," "disturbed," or even "psychotic." Every woman he dated suffered from some unresolved issue (usually anger) that made it impossible for her to form healthy relationships. And every one of them betrayed him in one way or another. Whenever he recounted one of his break-ups, his tone was so sad and soft-spoken that it would have been easy to believe that he in fact was the injured party. But we all knew through the community grapevine that women gave up the comfortable life he seemed to offer for the simple reason that he made them feel horrible about themselves. No one likes to be measured against an unattainable ideal. No one likes to feel that she cannot live up to criteria that are imposed on her from the outside. In addition, Ethan expected his partners to fit into his preexisting lifestyle. He had no interest in co-creating a future with a woman. Rather, he wanted her to slide into the life he already had. This ruled out all women with professional aspirations. And it excluded women who had a strong sense of their own individuality.

The situation was so drastic that the woman Ethan ended up marrying did not have any say about furnishing the house they lived in. The house, he told her, was "his." He had built it. She merely had the privilege of living in it. He even implied that she needed to earn her keep through household chores and yardwork. He expected his wife to "pay" for her wedding ring by her labor. When she suggested that she seek outside employment in order to contribute to their finances, he told her that it wasn't about money (which he had plenty of). It was a matter of principle: A wife should support her husband's overall vision of how his life was meant to be. No one was shocked when she left him less than a year after the wedding.

The women Ethan drove out reported, after the fact, that what made him so lethal was that he presented himself as a sensitive guy who wouldn't dream of mistreating a woman. He was a peace-loving environmentalist who made a point of stressing his abhorrence of abusive men. He even had an extensive collection of pop psychology titles that he had combed for morsels of psychobabble that he threw into the conversation whenever one of his girlfriends approached him with a relationship concern. He always spoke like the most rational man in the world, in a calm voice that signaled that he was "instructing" his partner in how to become a better person. He offered statements such as "there's no distinction between reasonable and unreasonable," "one shouldn't make any demands in a relationship," "we're all equally wounded," "no one can hurt you without your consent," "the only person who can undermine your confidence is you," and "it's not about what others do—it's about how you respond," etc.

Ethan pushed his girlfriends in this "gentle" manner until they snapped. And then he told them that *they* were the abusive ones. They were the ones raising their voice—the ones to fly off the handle without any reason. When the women finally left him, they were usually filled with rage about having been worn down by a man who was so good at covering his tracks that it was impossible to pin any guilt on him. After all, if a guy is convinced that there's no distinction between reasonable and unreasonable, you can never accuse him of having said or done anything unreasonable.

In one of my conversations with Ethan, he said a curious thing: "Women tend to feel diminished in relation to me." I was struck by his strange wording. He implied that the women he dated caused their own feelings of denigration—that he was merely a passive observer of their self-inflicted suffering. Ethan, in short, had no sense of his part in the tumultuous emotional dramas that surrounded him. Nor did he feel any responsibility for them. Women kept telling him that he was arrogant, patronizing, controlling, overly entitled, and self-centered. And he kept convincing himself that they only made these judgments because they were insecure or deranged. If they felt demeaned in relation to him, it was because they lacked self-esteem. What Ethan did not recognize was that his pattern of relating left the women in his life no space to be themselves. It left them no way to cultivate their distinctive spirit, or even to develop their interests in directions other than those dictated by his needs.

If you have ever dated a man like Ethan, you'll know that no matter how hard you try, you'll never be able to meet his needs. He's on a fervent quest for a woman who will complete the circle of his life. But because this woman is a figment of his imagination, no actual woman will ever satisfy him. He may initially revere you as the answer to his prayers. But the minute you assert your own personality, you'll disillusion him. The moment you reveal desires that fail to coincide with his image of you, he'll turn against you.

Women often blame themselves in such situations, trying to understand what they're doing wrong. They may even look for ways to "improve" themselves so as to fix the problem. But, in the end, there is not a lot to be done. The key to the situation resides with the narcissistic man. He is looking for a woman who is content to fulfill the role of a blow-up doll. The more fiercely self-sufficient you are, the more ruthlessly he'll seek to squash your spirit until you'll barely have enough strength to limp out of the relationship. And because no women can give this man what he wants, he'll keep moving from one woman to the next, convinced that somewhere "out there" is a woman who will truly understand him.

Narcissistic men rarely appreciate what they have in the present because they are focused on what "could" (or "should") one day come to pass. Because they bank on a fantasy that will never materialize, they keep themselves from fully stepping into the fold of the passing moment. The "commitment phobia" that some men cannot shake is one face of narcissistic love. It allows narcissistic men to hold the future open "just in case" the perfect woman comes along. These are also the men who are most likely to chase unavailable women. An elusive woman allows them to sustain their fantasy indefinitely. She remains a shimmering ideal—an object onto which a man can deposit all of his hopes without ever having to test them in real life. The more she tantalizes from a distance, the more persistently he pursues her. Until, of course, she allows herself to be "caught." That's when the narcissistic man's attention shifts to the next target. But before he leaves, he's likely to want to punish her for having wasted his time. In that case, he'll strive to devastate her before casting her aside like a used Kleenex.

3

A lot of Hollywood thrillers make brilliant use of this kind of narcissistic obsession. And no one does it better than Hitchcock. Take *Vertigo*. Much of the film consists of scenes where a private eye, Scottie, trails a mysterious woman called Madeleine. Scottie has been hired by Madeleine's husband to unlock her secrets, including the fact that she at times seems possessed by the restless spirit of a long-dead woman. As the plot thickens, we watch Scottie become increasingly spellbound with the aloof Madeleine. When Madeleine dies midway through the movie, he is so grief-stricken that he is confined to a mental institution. He's too catatonic to even recognize his close friend Midge—a woman who, like Hoffmann's Clara, can't compete with the fantasy object. Midge's love for Scottie is not enough to break Madeleine's hold. Yet Scottie hardly knew Madeleine. Hitchcock makes sure that the viewer understands that it's exactly because Madeleine remains a conundrum—a challenge to be over-come—that she wields such immense power over Scottie.

But Hitchcock doesn't stop here. He is pure genius at showing the brutality involved in turning a woman into a fantasy object. At a key turning point in the movie, we dis-cover that the elegant and upper-class Madeleine is in fact a working-class girl called Judy. Judy was hired to impersonate Madeleine to hide the fact that the real Madeleine has been coldly murdered by her husband. The "death" of Madeleine that Scottie witnessed was faked by Judy so that she would be released from the task of playing Madeleine indefinitely. The woman Scottie has been grieving with such passion was never Madeleine to begin with, but merely a fantasy that Judy performed for his benefit. After his release from the mental institution, Scottie spots Judy on the street. He instantly recognizes the resemblance between the two women. The trouble is that Judy is no longer Madeleine. Her clothes are too drab. Her hair color is all wrong. And her makeup is too vulgar. What does Scottie do? He sets out to transform Judy back into the refined Madeleine.

Shivers run down our spine as we watch Judy reluctantly step into Madeleine's stiletto heels, don Madeleine's classy suit, and, finally, dye and style her copper hair into Madeleine's impeccably coifed icy-blonde look. We are invited to witness the process by which Judy gets swallowed up by Scottie's fantasy (as Judy herself sums up the matter, "I don't care anymore about me"). But even this is not enough. Like Olympia, Judy is destroyed in the end of the movie. After her final attempt at playing Madeleine, she once again dies—this time for real. The lesson we learn is that when the fantasy object is beyond repair—when Scottie realizes that Judy can never be the Madeleine of his dreams—she must be eradicated. She only has value to the degree that she manages to embody his fantasy.

This is exactly the mentality of narcissistic men like Ethan. It explains why they often seek to take revenge on a woman who has slipped from her lofty pedestal. They become callous beyond comprehension because they can't stand the fall of their fantasy. They in fact can't tolerate the idea that there's something of you that might survive after they're done with you. Hitchcock knew this better than anyone.

That Hitchcock has "Madeleine" die three times in the film is meant to illustrate the persistent appeal of the fantasy object. It's meant to show that a man mesmerized by such an object will try to resurrect this object even if this entails relating to a false icon rather than an actual woman—even if it entails courting an Olympia rather than a Clara. Unfortunately, as women, we've been conditioned to play along. Without necessarily knowing when or how, we've been taught to act the part of the mysterious fantasy object.

Just think about what you do when you spot an enticing man at a party. Do you walk up to him and say, "Hi, I'm Kirsten. What brings you to this party?" Or do you craftily position yourself in his line of vision, copy the gestures of a woman having the time of her life, and hope that he'll make his way to you? We live in a culture that sees men as subjects who desire. And women as objects of that desire. Men get to look at us and want us while our job is to make ourselves as tempting (yet aloof) as possible. If men fantasize about winning the perfect object, women often fantasize about *being* that object. This is why many women prefer to be pursued rather than to pursue. And why women who choose to pursue often do so obliquely, by trying to induce their quarry to take the first step. They set the bait and hope for the best.

We've seen that self-help literature often explicitly tells women to do this. It instructs women to turns themselves into the perfect (hard to get) object. Instead of critiquing a cultural practice that is likely to attract the kinds of narcissistic guys I've been describing, it does everything in its power to buttress this practice. It sidesteps the fact that our willingness to "play Madeleine" feeds the self-centered tendencies of men who don't know how to love a woman for who she is. In addition, it makes it challenging for women to state their wants. If you're taught to see yourself as an object of male desire, it's difficult for you to think of yourself as someone who might actively want something from the world; it's hard to see yourself as a desiring agent.

One reason I'm so fond of the Nate Archibalds of the entertainment industry is that they are balancing the scales between men and women so that women also get to feast their eyes on some fantasy objects. But this is still far from leveling the playing field between men and women in the realm of real-life romance. In this realm, men are still likely to objectify women. And women are likely to thank them for it until the moment the fantasy shatters and the cruelty begins. This is why I think that self-help guides that teach women to personify a male fantasy are giving advice that is, arguably, deeply irresponsible.

4

Does this mean that we should give up trying to make ourselves desirable? Of course not! Desire is a scrumptious part of courtship. The art of seduction is one of life's biggest pleasures. And it usually includes aspects of fantasy. There's nothing wrong with this per se. It's just that we need to be careful about how seriously we take the fantasies that we devise. If we internalize the idea that we are desirable only when we manage to replicate the fantasy object, we are shooting ourselves in the foot. If we believe that our elaborate hairdo, body-hugging dress, three-inch heels, or sugary perfume are more important than the uniqueness of our spirit, we're in danger of losing ourselves in a fantasy. But if we retain a solid sense of where fantasy ends and our identity begins, things might not turn out as badly as they do for Judy (or Olympia).

This is where Cinderella can help us. At first glance, this girl with the famous glass slipper hardly seems to improve things for modern women. After all, what we find at the core of this fairy tale is a transformation scene not that different from what happens to Judy. With the help of a fairy godmother (and, in the Disney version, some suspiciously friendly mice and birds), Cinderella sheds her humble garb and steps into a gleaming gown so that she can attend the prince's opulent ball. It would be hard to argue that the prince falls in love with her inimitable spirit. Her glorious rise to a red-carpet sensation appears to be what does the trick.

Yet the prince doesn't turn away in disgust when Cinderella's castle-ready guise dissipates. It's the ash-covered girl in sackcloth that he proposes to. We're led to understand that somehow he's able to intuit what we already know, namely that Cinderella is a put-upon girl with a lot of strength, integrity, and ingenuity. Unlike other fairy-tale heroines such as Sleeping Beauty or even Snow White, Cinderella shows some real gumption. As to how the prince "knows" all of this remains a mystery. But this hardly matters in the make-believe world of magic wands and evil stepsisters. What matters is that when Cinderella gets her break, we are happy for her. And we trust that the prince marries her for the right reasons. We trust that he sees through the fantasy object to the heart of who she is.

Modern adaptations of Cinderella make the most of this. Contemporary romantic comedies, for instance, usually combine a titillating makeover scene with a story line that showcases the heroine's intelligence and independence. Think of the transformation of Julia Roberts from a hooker to a lady in *Pretty Woman*. Of Sandra Bullock from a crass FBI agent to a stunner in *Miss Congeniality*. Of Jennifer Lopez from a meek maid to a high-society looker in *Maid in Manhattan*. And of Anne Hathaway from a bushy-eyebrowed high-school nerd to a graceful princess in *The Princess Diaries*. Such makeover scenes appeal to the visual and sensory pleasure that women get from facials, haircuts, makeup, shoes, accessories, and such. They delight us because they suggest that, with just a little bit of work, any of us could become the perfect fantasy object. Yet the overall ethos of these movies is that the women getting dolled up are not pushovers. The movies take care to stress that their leading ladies would never let a guy forget who they are beneath the glam getup.

A skeptic might point out that these movies recycle an unfortunate idea that runs from Eve being forged out of Adam's rib to the Pygmalion story of Dr. Higgins and Eliza, namely that women are mere clay in the hands of men. The comical trials that Bullock and Hathaway undergo at the hands of the male experts hired to teach them the skills of feminine grooming support this interpretation. And, in *Pretty Woman*, it's Richard Gere's credit card and excellent taste in clothes and jewelry (not to mention his ability to spur snobbish sales personnel into fawning action) that accomplishes the miraculous overhaul of Roberts from a gum-chewing rebel to a polished connoisseur of polo matches and opera. When Gere escorts Roberts, clad in a stunning red gown, through the lobby of their hotel, all admiring eyes are on her. The message of the scene is clear: She has succeeded in becoming the fantasy object and he is to thank for the achievement.

If things were this simple, though, the movie wouldn't have been such a hit among female viewers. We are not masochistic. We wouldn't like the movie if we thought it showed Roberts as mere clay in the well-manicured hands of Gere.

The easiest way to understand why we don't is to compare the movie's emotional impact to that of *Vertigo*. Both movies include a lengthy scene where the male hero accompanies his female "project" on a shopping spree to pick up the right clothes and accessories. In *Pretty Woman*, Gere foots the bill for Roberts's transformation in exactly the same way as Scottie does for Judy in *Vertigo*. Yet we are not annoyed at him in the same way as we are at Scottie. Moreover, while we may gain some pleasure from witnessing Judy's (re)conversion into Madeleine, the scene is also uncomfortable to watch. We know that Judy's sense of self is being trampled on. She suffers and we suffer with her. *Pretty Woman*, in contrast, offers no such discomfort. Why not?

The answer is that, as viewers, we are introduced to Roberts's character long before she starts her transformation. We know that she's a small-town girl with big dreams and even bigger money troubles. She's loyal to her friends. She has a god-awful singing voice. She's not afraid to state her opinions. And she drives a stick-shift better than Gere ever will. No matter how much her appearance and demeanor change, we never lose track of the woman underneath the new look.

The same goes for Bullock in *Miss Congeniality*. Her antics at the beauty pageant can't make us forget that she snorts when she laughs, holds a demanding job at the FBI, downs a pint of Häagen-Dazs in one sitting, and knows how to defeat an assailant with four well-placed self-defense moves. Likewise for Lopez in *Maid in Manhattan* and Hathaway in *The Princess Diaries*. As opposed to Judy, whom we mostly know as the distant Madeleine, our modern heroines never entirely coincide with the fantasy of desirability they masquerade. The writers, directors, and producers of these movies have made sure that the fantasy aspects of the heroines are counterbalanced by their unmistakable humanity. And they have done this because they know that most female viewers won't pay up at the box office unless they feel empowered by the movies they watch.

5

Pretty Woman, Miss Congeniality, Maid in Manhattan, and *The Princess Diaries*, along with other hits such as *The Cinderella Story* (with Hilary Duff and Chad Michael Murray) and *Ever After* (with Drew Barrymore and Dougray Scott), are just the tip of the iceberg when it comes to Hollywood's passion for our favorite rags-to-riches fairy tale. Even the convoluted courtship of Elizabeth Bennett and Mr. Darcy in *Pride and Prejudice* falls under this rubric. We witness Elizabeth's climb from a family of modest means, questionable connections, and too many marriageable daughters to the arms of one of the richest noblemen of England. But what's so engaging about Elizabeth is that she doesn't let anyone—least of all the man she loves—weaken her independent spirit. She's the Lois Lane of the nineteenth century. And we also don't forget that she comes from a modest home. If Cinderella is one of the most enduring love stories of all time—one that we never tire of resurrecting—it's not merely because she appeals to our girlish dream of meeting a handsome prince on a white horse; it's because she's an ordinary girl who wrestles with some ordinary problems, such as being poor and having to put up with conceited and mean-spirited people. In *Pride and Prejudice*, the evil stepsisters are replaced by Mr. Bingley's haughty sister and her equally haughty upper-crust friends. In *Pretty Woman*, the stuck-up shop assistants step into this role. In *The Princess Diaries*, it's the snooty cheerleaders. Etc.

Cinderella's story sums up one of the most powerful daydreams of our time. Both the original fairy tale and its contemporary remakes reassure us that we can overcome adverse circumstances and triumph against all odds. Cinderella is the romantic counterpart to the working-class girl who gets into Yale, the struggling writer who writes a bestseller, the tongue-tied nerd who invents Microsoft and becomes a zillionaire, the mediocre student who discovers general relativity, the guy from the wrong side of the tracks who charms the admissions committee of Juilliard, the aging tennis player who wins Wimbledon, the underdog who gets the top job, and the skinny black lad from Hawaii who becomes president. She is the romantic version of the Nobody who becomes Somebody. This is as much a part of her appeal as her pumpkin carriage and midnight curfew. Those of us who are suspicious of the American Dream might find this a bit hard to swallow. But if we are willing to grant Will Smith his hour of happiness, why should we shun Cinderella? The girl deserves it!

The romantic comedies I've been talking about add yet another twist to all of this. The heroines of these movies get their guy. Being taught how to talk, walk, sit, and groom their eyebrows definitely helps. As do the amazing gowns. But, ultimately, the heroes of these movies come to their senses and claim their bride because she stays true to who she is. Much of this is done through easy-to-read metaphors, as is the way of Hollywood. But the message is still one that warms the hearts of modern women everywhere: Hold your ground and love will find you.

When Gere rides his white limo to Roberts's apartment, she's wearing jeans and has decided to return to her home town. When Agent Matthews (Benjamin Bratt) affirms Bullock's "You think I'm preeetty! You want to kiiiss me," she has reverted back to her bad-ass FBI persona. When Ralph Fiennes finally tracks down Lopez, she's back at the hotel kitchen. And the boy who gets to dance with Hathaway at the ball is not the one who only worships the princess she has become, but the one who adored her all along. Older examples of the theme include *Working Girl* and *An Officer and a Gentleman*. The surprisingly advanced lesson of these stories is that women want to be loved for who they are beyond the fantasy.

This is a lesson that narcissistic men like Ethan have yet to learn. These are some of the most dangerous men around. They'll only "love" you as long as you consent to wear your incandescent gown. Unlike Cinderella's prince—or the princes of romantic comedies—these guys won't propose to you after the clock strikes midnight and you turn back into a regular girl. They won't search the whole kingdom for your calloused foot. Instead, they'll belittle you for any and all displays of humanity. And they also won't understand that to love you means to make room for you in their lives. As far as they're concerned, your role is to mirror the life they have so carefully constructed. Don't be that mirror. Put on your Nikes and run out of the ball as fast as you can. The worst you could do would be to try to uphold their fantasy. You can't—not for long.

And don't forget that playing hard to get only makes it easier for these guys to objectify you. Sherry Argov would be horrified, but whenever I'm getting into a new relationship, I purposely make myself a little *more* available than I normally would be, just to see what the guy does. If he withdraws, chances are (1) he isn't that thrilled about dating me; (2) he's a caveman who needs to chase women in order to feel manly; or (3) he's a narcissist who is looking for a fantasy that has nothing to do with me. None of these options are of any interest to me. I figure that if I lose a guy like this, I won't be losing a whole lot. I want my partner to grasp the basic message of Cinderella, namely that there's a commoner underneath the princess getup. I want him to recognize that there's life after the ball—and that this life often falls short of even our most conservative fantasies.

CHAPTER 6

....

Why Playing Hard to Get Won't Work

MYTH: Playing hard to get increases your value.

FACT: Playing hard to get is what you do when you're not sure of your value.

1

I've shown that when playing hard to get works, it's usually for the wrong reasons, either because you're dealing with a guy who won't be that great for you in the long run, or because he's not that excited about dating you in the first place. It's now time to look at why this game won't work with quality guys.

First, though, I want to acknowledge that a degree of mystery can be attractive. But this is not because men are hunters. It's because people in general tend to be intrigued by the unknown. Women, like men, get curious about what eludes them. Women, like men, are likely to pay more attention to what is not easily attainable. When a potential partner throws him- or herself at us, it can be a turn-off for both genders. We're more likely to respond to someone who offers a slight challenge. It's in the nature of desire to intensify in the face of obstacles. It thrives on uncertainty. A little bit of fear will make the heart grow fonder. Longing and anticipation will fan the quiescent embers. But this is not a gendered phenomenon. It's hard for both men and women to wait until their object makes up his or her mind. It's difficult to sit on our hands when we would rather be tearing off someone's clothes. Let's not pretend that this is any easier for women than it is for men.

Other people are, by definition, partially opaque to us. Usually we don't give this a whole lot of thought. We don't need to know what the woman next to us on the bus is thinking. We don't even need to know what our coworkers, friends, parents, or neighbors are mulling over at any particular moment. But when it comes to lovers (or potential lovers), we're eager to infiltrate their innermost depths. In part this is because there is something reassuring about the idea that they don't hold anything back; we like to believe that there won't be any unpleasant surprises around the corner. But it's also because we're trained to think that the better we know our lover, the more intimate our relationship becomes. Knowledge, supposedly, opens to realms of togetherness that most of us covet but few of us attain. Our quest for knowledge, then, is not a matter of conquering our object. At least not primarily. It's a matter of being convinced that there is something he can give us—some satisfaction or transcendence—that we can't achieve on our own. As a result, a degree of unreadability is likely to pique our interest.

Yet most of us also worry about overstepping a boundary by coming on too strong. We're afraid that leaving that extra message or sending that extra email will make us seem too insistent, desperate, or disrespectful. We usually pull back when we get no response. Or when the response is too long in coming or too curt. This is exactly why playing hard to get won't work with most quality guys. They are as unlikely to pursue someone reluctant as you are because, like you, they don't want to be overbearing. They don't want to embarrass themselves by chasing a woman who isn't interested. If you keep thinking that men are hunters, you can easily overlook this. But if you remind yourself that most guys are a lot like you, you'll immediately see that the sane ones won't pursue you without explicit encouragement.

Most guys have a strong sense of the line between interest and stalking. If they are at all fearful that they might be close to crossing this line to the side of stalking, they'll back away immediately. While there are some aggressive types who will pursue you even after you discourage them by your silence, these are probably not the men you'll want to date. I expect you've had at least one experience with a man who refused to be shaken even though you kept ignoring him. My guess is that his persistence didn't do much for him—that you became more and more exasperated over time. You might have even rolled your eyes at his latest email. Nice guys know this. They would much rather err on the side of caution than risk being thought of as a crazy stalker. Whenever a female friend tells them about some creep who won't leave her alone, they make a mental note never to give any woman reason to talk about them that way.

2

On a deeper level, playing hard to get won't work because it's a corrupt attempt to feign self-possession. The intuition behind it is correct. It recognizes that most people find it easier to love someone who takes responsibility for his or her life than someone whose entire universe revolves around them. People are strange creatures in that they want to feel free even when they're attached. When they think that they might have the power to devastate their lover, they're likely to back away before they get a chance to use that power. This is not necessarily because they're uncaring or afraid of being caged. It's just that being asked to guarantee another person's welfare is more than most people can handle. It's too scary.

Imagine how you would react if a guy you were dating revealed that his life would fall to pieces if you chose to leave. You might withdraw immediately to make sure that things didn't get out of hand. Or you might stay but not be able to shake the feeling of impending catastrophe. Obviously, if you're in a committed relationship, you'll know that you have a lot of power over your partner. This is what commitment means, in part. But when you're just starting out in a relation-ship, the terror of devastating your partner can hinder your ability to relish the relationship. The same applies to men.

Self-help authors know this. They know that a man who

believes that you have enough self-possession to lead a sat-isfying life without him is less likely to flee than one who is afraid that he might end up toppling your world. This is why they advocate playing hard to get. They want you to have an appearance of self-possession. They might even instruct you to yawn and look at your watch every time your boyfriend alludes to the future (or brings up the topic of marriage). However, most guys are not this gullible. They'll see through the ruse (in part because they expect it). They'll know you're merely fabricating self-reliance. The fact that you feel the need to resort to games only confirms this. What's more, this strategy is always a short-term "solution" at best. After all, if you want to be with a guy, eventually you'll need to make yourself available.

Authentic self-possession incites admiration. When you live your life to the fullest, you're desirable. When you nur-ture your spirit, you're lovable. When you're self-sufficient, you're hotter than your grandpa's wood stove. But this can't be faked. Self-possession is not about counting the days until you return a call, or about intentionally keeping a guy guessing when you've already made up your mind. It's about having an inner reservoir of self-reliance. This core of com-posure can't be forged. Game-playing can only degrade it. You either have it or you don't. A quality guy will recognize the difference between a hoax and the real thing. Perhaps not immediately, but it won't take him too long. And he'll walk away from the fake because, like you, he wants the real thing. A jerk might want to play with the fake for a while before he tosses you out. Like a cat tormenting a half-dead mouse, he might give you a few rounds of attention before moving on. But a quality guy won't even do that. He won't have much interest in a woman who is willing to play the part of a half-dead mouse.

Women are taught that making a guy work for it raises their value. But I think that the very opposite is the case—that nothing signals lack of confidence more than the idea that you need to manipulate a lover in order to keep his interest. Real self-possession is a matter of knowing that you have something precious to offer to the right guy, and that you don't need to pretend anything to attract this guy. Playing hard to get is the weak girl's strategy. It's a strategy you resort to when you're not sure that you're good enough as you are. If you're truly convinced of your worth, you'll know you're good enough. If you're filled with purpose and positive energy, you'll know that you're a great catch. And you won't need to put any effort into tricking a guy into thinking the same. When you are genuinely the mistress of your own life, you won't be afraid to play your cards without cheating. Equally importantly, you won't be afraid to fly solo until the right guy comes along. You'll actually mean it when you tell a man that you only want him if he wants you.

This can be hard for many women because our culture makes us nervous about being single. The pop songs we hear in department stores and elevators tell us that being single is the worst thing that could ever happen to us. "Scientific" studies inform us that single women are lonely, empty, depressed, and miserable. They're almost less than human—somehow incomplete or unfinished. Never mind that many women who are coupled up feel emotionally depleted. That many relationships are confining and mind-numbing. Or that some are even overtly traumatizing. Singleness is still, in comparison, supposedly a state to be avoided at all costs. We're told that if we fall into it, we should try to overcome it as fast as possible. We're in fact so programmed to pursue relationships that we often settle for extremely mediocre ones. In such cases, love becomes merely a way of fending off the "tragedy" of singleness. Rather than explore the rewards of self-sufficiency—such as the chance to cultivate parts of our being that thrive in solitude—we prefer to stake our happiness on love, no matter how lukewarm this "love" might be. Sometimes we even get so paralyzed that we stay in a hurtful relationship.

It's worth reminding yourself that singleness has its advantages. For one thing, it allows you to become better acquainted with yourself. It allows you to familiarize yourself with aspects of your being that shy away from the company of others. You might even discover sources of creativity that you never knew you had. Many people who have truly distinguished themselves in our society have been single for long stretches of their lives. Often solitude is a precondition of achievement. I'm not saying that you shouldn't value relationships. It's just that when your fear of being alone is greater than your determination to make it on your own, you may end up compromising your potential. Periods of solitude rarely steal your power. Rather, they recharge you when you are in danger of getting exhausted by too many social demands. They may even replenish your capacity for more profound interpersonal alliances. They may help you stockpile vitality that you'll need when you once again enter into the whirlwind of relationships.

3

Being able to tolerate periods of singleness is the flipside of high-quality relationships. It's impossible to love fully without risking aloneness. When you wager everything, you take the chance of falling from higher than when you wager nothing. And aloneness, as we know, is what comes after the fall. So if you want to love with the kind of ardor that pierces your being, the first thing you'll need to overcome is your terror of singleness. There's no way to anchor your relationship into a calm cove that's completely sheltered from Cupid's temper tantrums. Sometimes things fall apart when you least expect it; sometimes you don't see the storm coming. Other times, the thunder clouds hang low for a long time before the storm breaks. Either way, there will be times when shelter is nowhere to be found. So you weather the storm. You wait for better days. Alone.

Knowing that you have the resilience to carry on alone doesn't make love any easier. But it will gain your lover's respect. And it allows you to set the bar high. It keeps you from being willing to accept less than what meets your needs. Think of this as the strong woman's version of playing hard to get. When you set the bar high, you genuinely *are* "hard to get" in the sense that you know that you merit a guy's best effort. You don't play hard to get in order to (artificially) make yourself desirable. Rather, you are desirable because you (genuinely) *are* hard to get. It's not a game. It's a state of mind that allows you to opt for singleness over unsatisfying relationships.

In a way, "playing hard to get" and "setting the bar high" aim at the same goal. It's just that the former arises from insecurity while the latter is a sign of authentic self-sufficiency. Some women struggle with this because self-sufficiency can sometimes seem uncomfortably close to selfishness. And, selfishness, we all know, does not sit well with our cultural ideals of femininity. If anything, women have been taught to make themselves small, to expect very little, to ask for even less, and to yield to the desires of others whenever they can; they've been taught to put the needs of others ahead of their own.

To be demanding is not feminine. To reach high is not womanly. On the one hand, we're told that men love defenseless women—that the best way to gain a man's affection is to play a little helpless. On the other, we're told that there's nothing that turns a man off faster than "feminine" neediness. This usually translates to saying that we shouldn't have any emotional needs at all. The contradiction is blatant. We're encouraged to pretend that we don't know how to change the light bulb. *This* kind of "neediness" will supposedly awaken men's protective instincts. But emotional needs? Those are a no-no. Can't have those. They'll drive a guy out of our lives faster than a fistful of bedbugs.

I've always found this contradiction baffling. Why is it that neediness in the practical sense is supposed to turn men on whereas the slightest sign of emotional neediness is supposed to turn them off? Why is it that my fleeting moment of sadness will send a man running but my inability to hang a picture will draw him closer? The explanation we're usually given is that men feel helpful when it comes to concrete actions, but that they feel at a loss with emotions. By now you'll know that I have little patience with this explanation. I trust that most modern men process emotions just as well as women do. The insistence that they don't is merely a convenient way to convince women that we shouldn't expect emotional answerability from our men.

Meeting the mess of other people's emotions is difficult for all of us. I am reminded of this every time a student walks into my office in a state of apprehension or wretchedness about something that's keeping him from turning his paper in on time. It would be expedient if I could pretend that I don't comprehend his feelings. But I'm not going to be that lazy. And I'm certainly not going to be that lazy with a man I love. Why, then, should he be able to hide behind some feeble rationalization about men being hopeless dimwits when it comes to emotions?

Self-sufficiency doesn't mean that we have no needs. It means that we know that these needs are important. Let's make sure that we don't buy into either cultural or self-help

attempts to persuade us otherwise. Let's not reconcile ourselves to dating men who don't understand us. Or who can't
even be bothered to try. Let's not sell ourselves short just
because we think that we don't have the right to ask for more.
But let's also recognize that there will be times when our
needs won't be met. There will be lows. There will be tough
passages. There will be times when we'll feel lonely—when
the price of self-sufficiency seems too high. But in the long
run, our chances of attracting the right man are much higher
if we insist on keeping the bar high.

Whenever a guy fails to clear our bar, we have two choices.
We can lower our bar. Or we can take it elsewhere. I recommend picking up that bar and carrying it to the next hot guy
who crosses your path. Not only will this give you a chance to
get what you want, but it will spare you the mortification of begging for something that you can't have. It will release you from
the prolonged agony of always getting less than you ask for.

4

Let's be clear about something. There's a difference between
refusing to play hard to get on the one hand and flinging
yourself at guys who don't want you on the other. The fact
that you don't want to "play Madeleine" doesn't mean that
you should offer yourself to guys who can't get that enthusiastic about you. It doesn't mean that you should do all
the work and pursue someone who seems vague, reluctant,
distant, or indifferent. I couldn't care less about who makes

the first move. But if a guy isn't meeting you halfway, it's time to reassess the situation. Ditto if he isn't treating you with respect. What's the point of running after someone who doesn't return your passion? You can't cajole him into loving you. Indeed, if he doesn't feel that way about you, he can't force himself even if he wanted to. And you sure can't make him. This truly is a relationship cul-de-sac. It's best to accept defeat and move on.

This can be tough, particularly when the guy's promising. But it's actually great news. It means that there's nothing to stop you from setting your bar as high as you wish. The guys who don't want you aren't worth your attention. And the ones who do will do their best to clear your bar. You won't need to stoop to game-playing to ensure this. All you'll need is a good sense of what you want from a relationship.

You want that ring on your finger? So be it. That's what you should ask for. You don't much care about the ring, but would like a partner who is able to hear you out no matter what? So be it. The point is to decide what it is that you want. There is no formula—no right way to love or be loved. There's only what you and your partner choose to build between yourselves. It makes no difference who called whom first, who cooks dinner, mows the lawn, makes more money, hails a cab, initiates sex, or navigates the grid of highways in Providence, RI (whoever is able to find Connecticut deserves a medal). And it definitely makes no difference who changes the light bulb. If your relationship works, it works. If it doesn't, look for one that does.

This simplifies things, doesn't it? Either a guy is willing to clear your bar, or he doesn't like you enough to exert himself. In the latter case, playing hard to get and other such parlor games may help you spark his interest. But sooner or later, that interest will waver. It will move onto some other woman who either plays the game better than you do, or whose bar is lower than yours. This is why having the strength to pick up that bar and carry it elsewhere is a thousand times more valuable than knowing all the right games. Which, again, is not to say that picking up the bar is easy. It takes a lot of self-confidence. It takes a degree of fearlessness about the future. There's no shortcut that will let you bypass the fact that your most pressing mission in life is to garner all the self-confidence and fearlessness that you can muster. This may take some time. It may require some soul-searching. It may even demand some concrete sacrifices, such as investing a few years in your education so that you can climb up the career ladder, improve your income, and have a room of your own.

I know from personal experience that it's easy to under-estimate the importance of tangible things like these. I grew up poor. My parents have no education beyond elementary school. Arriving at Brown at the age of eighteen was a humbling experience. Going against the prep school kids made me think I was going to flunk out my first semester. And even with generous scholarships, I accumulated a lot of debt. Harvard tripled this debt. I lived in constant terror of financial disarray. Whenever a romantic relationship ended, my partner was likely to tell me that it was because I was too self-doubting. For a long time, I kept thinking that this was a psychological issue. I spent years in therapy trying to sort it out. But then I landed a prestigious job, secured a sizable income, published a couple of books, got tenure, paid back my loans, bought a house, and—frankly—became a different person. It felt almost miraculous. My relationships changed. I no longer feel that I'm bargaining from a position of weakness. If things go wrong, it's definitely not because I'm too self-doubting.

The practical details of your life can have a tremendous impact on your overall self-esteem and sense of security. They can determine what you deem you have a right to expect from your relationships. When you feel that you can't quite measure up to the guy you're dating in terms of income or accomplishments, things can get tricky.

My friend, Crystal, is a case in point. She has a pleasant but low-paying job in a major department store. She recently dated a venture capitalist who makes about $600,000 a year. He convinced Crystal that because of the discrepancy between their incomes, he should pay for everything. Crystal let him, in part because he made it clear that he wasn't going to change his lifestyle just to date her. When he selected restaurants that cost more than her weekly income, she didn't complain. And when he ordered a $200 bottle of wine, she didn't argue. From his perspective, none of this was a big deal. He could afford it. And, in any case, he had an expense account. He didn't think that Crystal owed him anything.

But *she* did. She couldn't help but feel that she was some-how obliged to him. As a result, it was much more difficult for her to stand up to him when they had a disagreement. It was harder for her to make an emotional request of any kind. Because he gave her so much, materially speaking, she felt that she didn't have the right to ask for anything else. The relationship disintegrated in part because there was an imbalance—a basic inequality—between them.

We've seen that some self-help authors will tell you that insisting on equality will destroy your chances for romance. But I think that relationships are much more likely to fail when there's some sort of an obvious disparity between the partners. A few decades ago, it was common for highly educated and wealthy men to be married to women who didn't have the same credentials or earning power. Things have changed. I'm by no means saying that your relation-ship will only work if you have the same level of schooling or professional status as your boyfriend or husband. I'm not talking about balancing the scales quite so crudely. But if you let things get too unequal—if you keep yielding to your guy because you feel that you owe him something—you'll have a harder time at it.

5

The opposite of this are guys who think that they deserve to lord it over you because they make more money or have a bigger house than you do. Ethan from the previous chapter is one of these men. As you may recall, he wanted his wife to earn her keep. I don't meet these kinds of men too often. But when I do, I'm astonished. I'm stunned that there are men who still approach relationships with the idea that a woman who can't match their income must make up for it in other ways—be it through unpaid labor or meek submission or runway-ready beauty.

Every time you manage to pick up your bar and walk away from a guy like this, you'll be able to put some more confidence in your piggy bank. There's nothing better for your self-esteem than having the strength to reject what you know is bad for you. This goes for potato chips and pizza, but it also goes for certain kinds of men. The more times you turn your back on a guy who treats you like a second-class citizen, the more self-possessed you'll grow. And the bonus is that you increase the likelihood of meeting a man who is right for you. Weeding out the questionable guys will create room for this man.

Best of all, you now have an efficient way to tell the quality guys from the questionable ones. The quality guys don't need you to play hard to get. *They won't back away just because you're available.* The questionable ones might. But since you don't want them anyway, you have absolutely nothing to lose. If you suspect you might have found Mr. Right, give him a call. If he actually *is* Mr. Right, he won't be so stupid as to reject you just because you picked up the phone.

Even if you can't immediately replace all the false starts with Mr. Right, you'll gain something from pushing the false starts out of your life. You'll gain a peace of mind. You'll learn that you're able to do just fine without a man at your side. At first glance, this may seem like the short end of the stick. But when you think about it, wouldn't you rather be content and alone than miserable with some guy who expects you to mop his floors because you don't have a trust fund?

When there's no one to suggest that you're not good enough or feminine enough or helpless enough or sexy enough or beautiful enough or whatever enough, you might actually start to feel pretty good about yourself. When no one is measuring you against external standards, you might get around to devising your own set of values. You might start to compare yourself not to what some guy wants you to be but an ideal of your own devising. And then you can get to work at gradually closing the gap between your present state and your ideal state. You're unlikely to ever completely close that gap. That's okay. We're not Olympians. We can't expect perfection from ourselves. But we can work toward something more compelling, as long as we're the ones to set the standards.

When it comes to romance, there's nothing as powerful as being able to draw a line in the sand and say, "This is acceptable; that's not." When your relationship saps your spirit—or when you're overwhelmed by feelings of sadness or inadequacy—it's time to take a good look at that line and to make sure that you're still standing on the right side of it.

Self-possession is not a matter of playing hard to get to convince a guy of your worth. It's a matter of having enough self-reliance to choose singleness over a demeaning relationship.

Every time. A quality man will admire this because he knows that this kind of self-certainty is a sign of authentic strength. He knows that if you choose to keep him in your life, it's because you relish his company. And he'll do everything he can to keep things that way. He'll meet you halfway, in part because he knows that anything less will end the relationship, but in large part because he knows he has landed the deal of a lifetime. What could be better than a woman who stays with him even though she's powerful enough to walk away at any moment? What could be more wonderful than a woman who will let him be free because she's confident that he'll never find anyone more engaging? Nothing. Quality men know this. And so should you.

PART II

....

Changing How We Think
about Love and Romance

....

CHAPTER 7

It's All about the Thing

> **MYTH:** Love at first sight shouldn't be trusted—it's misleading and treacherous.
>
> **FACT:** Instant attraction can be an uncannily accurate gauge of romantic compatibility.

1

Have you ever wondered why you want Tom rather than Jack, even when Jack is hotter than Tom? Or even when Jack has more money, power, property, and prestige (all the Helen Fisher markers of masculine desirability)? If so, you might be interested in what one of my favorite thinkers—the French psychoanalyst Jacques Lacan—has to say. Lacan explains that when we're attracted to someone, it's not his list of accomplishments that captivates us, but rather something called "the Thing." The capital T is important here because this is not any old "thing" (say, an old shoe or even a Harry Winston emerald necklace). I'm talking about the enigmatic Thing your deepest desires are made of.

If you're a woman who worships money, power, property,

and prestige, these factors may come to stand for your Thing. But usually the Thing is much less tangible than this. Usually it's not something you can designate. Yet you know when a man has it. It draws you magnetically. It trumps all the other things in the world because you (unconsciously) think that once you find it, all your problems will magically disappear. You believe that acquiring this Thing will heal all of your wounds and make you feel whole again.

But why do you feel wounded in the first place? Lacan explains that all of us do. We all feel lacking in one way or another. Here's why. When we're first born into the world, we can't tell the difference between ourselves and the rest of the world. We can't, for instance, distinguish between ourselves and our mother. It takes us a while to realize that the world is much bigger than our own limited reality—that we're just a tiny boat bobbing on an enormous ocean. What's more, this demotion from being the belly-button of the world to being merely a small sliver of its colossal pie comes at a cost: We recognize that we don't rule the world. *Ouch!* If our mother walks out of the room, we can scream all we want. But we can't force her to come back. We also can't force her to feed us, pick up our toys, sing to us, or smile at us. If we're lucky enough to have a nice mom, she'll do these things anyway. But we can't *make* her. And this goes for other people in our lives as well. Double ouch! We can learn to manipulate our little brother into sharing his jelly beans. But we can't make him. At least not without pulling his hair. But if we pull his hair, our mother will stop smiling at us. Thus we learn one of the most basic lessons of life: You win some, you lose some. We learn that we're not omnipotent—that, all things considered, we are fairly insignificant. That's why we feel lacking.

Lacan's story recycles an ingenious plot from the Bible: First there's Paradise. Then there is the Fall. You take one bite of a shiny apple and suddenly you're a sinner. The main difference is that instead of running away from sex, as the Bible would have you do, you'll be running after it for the rest of your life. This is because you think that sex has the power to return you to Paradise. Which, of course, it does. But only momentarily. The annoying thing is that you can't stay there. You can't set up permanent residency in the Paradise of Sex. As much as you try to resist the gravitational pull of the earth, you always in the end fall into a portal that dumps you back in the middle of your worldly affairs. Your Paradise Lost will, unfortunately, remain irrevocably lost. This is why you feel as if you had been cheated out of some incomparably precious Thing.

By the time we hit puberty, we know we don't have the Thing. We know life is unfair. And we definitely know we're not invincible. This feeling of being somehow less than complete endures throughout our lives, creating a vague undercurrent of dissatisfaction that murmurs beneath our everyday concerns. Its intensity ebbs and flows. There are times when we're barely aware of it. Other times, it turns into a rapidly encroaching lava flow that just about buries us alive. However, most of us are extremely good at blotting it out. We can go for long stretches without thinking about it too much. Often we distract ourselves by getting super-busy. Having noisy children of our own may help, as may other life ambitions. Yet we can never completely suppress it. Those who stay preoccupied with it are often chronically sad (or even suicidal). Sometimes, they become writers, thera-pists, intellectuals, or philosophers—folks who devote their lives to understanding what it means that at the very heart of human experience is a void. Jean-Paul Sartre called this void "nothingness." Lacan called it "lack." I call it the silent sob underneath my breastbone. You may have your own name for it. But you probably know exactly what I'm talking about.

What makes this inner void so difficult to deal with is that it's amorphous. We can't fix it because we can't pinpoint its precise cause. And even if we could, we wouldn't be able to banish it. It's the price we pay for being human. The best we can do is to find ways to compensate for it. We can build careers, families, friendships, and gym-toned bodies. We can amuse ourselves with books, magazines, movies, *American Idol*, Tyra Banks, golf, George Clooney, indie rock, knitting patterns, or the poker tables of Las Vegas. We can write, paint, sculpt, dance, make music, take photos, or grow organic veg-etables. We can stalk people on Facebook, MySpace, Twitter, or YouTube. We can lose hours of our day in the quagmire of Google. Some of us get addicted to crack, heroin, Napa Valley Cabernet, French fries, Twinkies, Twix bars, computer games, Tom Welling, or anything written by Aaron Sorkin. *Law and Order* (despite not being written by Sorkin) is always a good bet because it's super-easy to get ahold of whenever we need a fix.

If all of this isn't enough to silence the dull echo within our hollow inner chamber, we can always daydream about the perfect Fendi bag, Cartier bracelet, Valentino dress, or Victoria Beckham's platform shoes (or her husband's washboard abs, if that's what we're in the mood for). And most of us are intimately familiar with the deeply beneficial effects of retail therapy. Even if it's just a trip to the hardware store, there can be something strangely satisfying about tossing that bag of nails into the trunk of our beat-up Subaru.

It's not difficult to figure out what's going on. We stuff one thing after another into the lack within our being in the hope of filling it. The practitioners of Zen Buddhism—along with other meditative folks—are not afraid to confront this lack head-on. But the rest of us need to cloak it with whatever diversions we can find.

This is not necessarily a bad thing. Many of the greatest achievements of humankind—not to mention of our own lives—owe their existence to this quest to alleviate a fundamental human malaise. If chimps have not yet invented a working elevator, it's because they (presumably) don't suffer from this malaise. We, however, are driven to create, imagine, fabricate, collect, and organize things because we are looking for a suitable substitute for the lost Thing (a.k.a. our sense of wholeness). The very fact that none of the objects we meet in the world can fully match the sparkle of what we think we have lost only guarantees that we'll keep amassing new objects; it guarantees that we'll keep devising fresh goals and aspirations.

The things of the world are always merely a pale reflection of the original lost Thing. They can only give us a faint trace of what we really want. This doesn't mean that they don't please us at all. Many of them give us immense satisfaction. It's just that our satisfaction is never complete. We always want more. In the same way that you might want a few spoonfuls of your date's pecan pie even after you've stuffed yourself with crème brûlée, you're likely to create new desires the minute your old ones are fulfilled. The moment you land a good job you start looking for a better one. And now that you've finally been able to buy a Toyota, you begin to dream about a BMW. You found the perfect outfit at H&M? This only makes you more jealous of the exclusive boutiques of Rodeo Drive and Madison Avenue. Your boyfriend took you to a lovely B&B at Lake Tahoe for your birthday? Maybe next year he'll fly you to Shanghai. There's no end to human desire. The more we get, the more we want. This is why those looking for spiritual enlightenment often give up their belongings or cloister themselves in monasteries with nothing to distract them. They know that the best way to kill desire is to feed it nothing at all.

2

What does this have to do with love? You guessed it! There's absolutely nothing in the world that comes closer to filling the hole within our being than the person we love. This person is our best imaginable line of defense against feeling incomplete. We've seen that narcissistic guys like Ethan will exploit this defense to the point of hurting the women they date. This is regrettable. But we might as well admit that we're all tempted to use love as a means of self-fulfillment.

Usually, we won't take things as far as Ethan does. Usually we're able to snap out of our fantasy before it ruins our chances for intimacy. But there's no use in denying that when we fall madly in love, we feel whole again. Our lack recedes to the background so that, for the time being at least, we feel elated, vibrantly alive, heady with delight, and full of potential. Our life finally has meaning. The minor stresses and annoyances of the daily grind retreat from our path. The pavement under our Jimmy Choo heels welcomes our springy stride. The sea of our anxieties parts at one flick of our magic wand. Our words ring with wisdom we didn't know we possessed (Napa Valley Cabernet helps). We have become the perfect blend of Hillary Clinton and Halle Berry: We can accomplish anything we want. We are no longer a tiny boat on a turbulent sea; we're an ocean liner on a minuscule pond. What *Titanic*? What lack? Our insurance policy covers not only shipwreck but also any and all misplaced Things.

Falling in love makes us feel as if we finally had the Thing. Even though in our more lucid moments we know that the man in question is a flawed and careworn person like everyone else, the initial rush of love makes us feel so redeemed that it's hard for us not to idolize him. Lacan has a catchy slogan for this: We raise our lover to "the dignity of the Thing." We assign to him the dignity—the nobility and incomparable worth—of our most coveted object. The poor guy won't know what hit him! Except that if he feels the same way about us, he's busy worshipping at the altar he has hastily put together for us. Both men and women feel the need to venerate the person who seems to be handing them the missing piece of their life-puzzle. This makes sense, right? It makes sense to assume that the person who is promising to take us back to Paradise is a little godlike.

Too good to be true? You bet. Even if we manage to side-step the excesses of Ethan's destructive narcissism, we're still asking a mere mortal to do the job of a god. We're asking Mr. Cupcake for something he's absolutely incapable of delivering, for there is no way that he—or anyone else—can complete our being. I know this is hard to accept. I routinely convince myself that Tom Welling *could* do it if he really wanted to. But the sad truth is that, as convincingly as a guy may evoke the Thing, he can't, in the end, deliver it to our doorstep.

The reason for this is that the fantasy of the Thing is a bunch of hogwash to begin with. It's not like we ever actually were omnipotent. It's not like we once had Paradise and then lost it. To be blunt about it: We never had the damned Thing in the first place. We just like to think so. Which, in turn, means that asking a guy to incarnate the Thing is like asking for snow in Central Park during one of those sweltering August days that sends New Yorkers to their air-conditioned closet-sized apartments (or to the Hamptons, if you're one of the lucky ones). You might think that you can get around the problem by marrying one of those über-rich guys on the

Upper East Side who can afford a snow machine. But no. Snow machine or no snow machine, there isn't a man in the world who can return to you a wholeness that you never had in the first place.

3

Feeling incomplete is part of the human condition. There's no cure. One reason the sport of playing hard to get is so seductive is that it allows us to circumvent this fact. It delays the moment when we must admit that Mr. Cupcake is not going to release us from our misery. As long as we keep him at arm's length, we can trick ourselves into thinking that he contains the Thing we so desperately crave. And our cat-and-mouse game makes it possible for him to keep thinking the same about us. As long as we elude his grasp, he doesn't know us very well. And as long as he doesn't know us very well, he can keep projecting his wildest fantasies onto us. In a sense, we actively invite him to act like Ethan. We voluntarily become his Thing: The muse who releases the genius within him; the virgin who makes all the badness of the world disappear; the whore who fulfills his most wanton erotic longings; the mother who smooths away his wrinkles of worry; and the Statue of Liberty who graciously welcomes him into a country where his "pursuit of happiness" will be taken very seriously indeed.

With such expectations in place, is it any wonder when things fall apart at the first glimmer of reality? The Thing doesn't have weaknesses. Trying to live up to it will exhaust even the perkiest of girls. And this dynamic isn't any easier for men. We can inflict exactly the same kind of pressure on them.

The more we elevate a guy to the dignity of the Thing, the less fallible we allow him to be. Lacan has a clever way to describe this. He explains that whenever a man becomes a Thing for us, what we want from him is something "more than" him. Our desire fixates on a mysterious kernel of desirability that we ourselves plant within him. This kernel is, literally, "more than" him because it originates from us. We of course don't realize this. We keep thinking that the guy's appeal is his own doing—that he's so sexy or fascinating because he's somehow better than the rest of them. We fail to see that it's our own desire that's turning him into Orlando Bloom.

Women complain all the time how taxing it is to live up to the impossible ideals of desirability that circulate in our culture. It's demoralizing to meet airbrushed waifs every-where we look. Whether these images stare at us from the pages of *Vogue*, the muddy flanks of a passing city bus, or the heights of a Times Square billboard, they eat away at our self-confidence. They wear down our defenses so that, at the end of the day, we run into Barney's in search of the anti-aging cream or lash-enhancing mascara that will make us look a bit more like those women. And we (rightly) berate the men in our lives whenever they buy into these ideals.

Imagine what it would feel like if your boyfriend told you one day that he has booked you a makeover session at Saks so that you can look more like Matthew McConaughey's gor-geous girlfriend. First you would tell him that even Matthew

McConaughey's girlfriend can only look like Matthew McConaughey's girlfriend after she has been electronically nipped and tucked by someone skilled at photo-finishing. Then you would tell him that Matthew McConaughey's girlfriend is called Camila Alves—something your boyfriend would know if he bothered to think of her as a person rather than mere arm-candy. And, finally, you would tell him that even though you agree that Camila Alves is attractive, you don't have any burning desire to become her clone.

It's good to keep in mind that when you turn a guy into a Thing, you're engaged in something similar to this scenario. It's just that your comparison point is not Camila Alves, but rather the mystifying kernel of your own desire. Since you yourself have a difficult time deciphering this kernel, you can hardly expect your guy to be able to do so. And, in any case, it would be unreasonable to ask him to refashion his whole being to match the quirks of your desire.

The only way to avoid being sucked into such la-la land of wish-fulfillment is to get to know your guy as a multidimensional entity. You need to make sure that there are basic qualities about him that you appreciate (such as honesty, integrity, or responsibility). This doesn't mean that you have to completely give up the Thing. You just need to put it in its place so that it doesn't take up all the space between you and your man. The Thing, however enticing, can only be one aspect of your relationship—an aspect that shouldn't eclipse the substance of your time together. It's merely the cherry on top of your ice-cream sundae. It adds a dash of flamboyance to the sundae. But if you only had the cherry without the sundae, you would hardly be satisfied.

4

But why do you need the cherry in the first place? Isn't it largely superfluous? If the Thing is such a nuisance, why not just get rid of it? The short answer is that you can't: It's not a matter of willpower. The more complicated answer is that the Thing is what makes love so uniquely entrancing. It would be easy to assume that the Thing's illusory character makes it irrelevant. But it isn't. It's what passion is woven of. It's what gives that special *je ne sais quoi* to your love. Your relationship needs honesty, integrity, and responsibility. But it also needs the aura of the Thing.

I already mentioned that the mundane substitutes you find for your missing Thing often give you enormous pleasure. From the Valentino dress to that bag of nails, the objects that make up for the lack of the Thing render your life more rewarding. Likewise, the fact that your guy can't return your Thing to you doesn't mean that you were mistaken to detect an echo of this Thing in him. Admitting that the Thing is unattainable doesn't mean that you can't bask in its glow. Or that your guy isn't the source of this glow. In the same way that the ocean can reflect the rays of the moon without being the moon, a man can reflect the rays of your fantasy Thing without being that Thing. That's why he has the power to usher you to the edge of transcendence.

If you want to avoid Ethan's narcissistic trap, you can't equate your guy with the Thing. Yet it would be dishonest to pretend that the Thing is not in the mix. You're not engaged in a Thing-or-nothing game. You can have your sundae and eat your cherry too. Or, to use another analogy, the Thing is like the fragile Wentworth china that you take out on special occasions. You can't put it in the dishwasher. In terms of everyday life, it's more or less useless. But this doesn't mean that you should throw it out. It's still one of the best parts of your holidays. It would be foolish to completely displace it by some durable everyday dishes.

Ethan's problem is that he thinks that everyday dishes leave no space for Wentworth china—that once a lover reveals herself to be less than ideal, she no longer contains the Thing. He doesn't understand that the everyday and the Thing are not always mutually exclusive. That a woman can be at once an imperfect creature and the Thing of his dreams. This short-sightedness makes it difficult for him—and for others like him—to sustain relationships beyond the early stages of infatuation.

Let me put the matter in yet another way. Even though the Thing can prompt you to have unrealistic expectations, it's not a misreading. It's definitely not the whole truth about a man. But it's not totally false either. If anything, it helps you dive beneath a man's façade to locate the unique spirit that speaks to your desire. The Thing is not synonymous with this spirit. Yet it has an uncanny ability to lead you directly to it. It can escort you straight to the most engaging part of a given man.

This is because your investments are not random. Even though it's you who brings your desire to a specific man, there's still an unconscious logic to your selections. It's not every man you choose to turn into a Thing. There's always something about him that elicits your curiosity. Often enough this is a nebulous quality—a vibe rather than a specific characteristic. But sometimes it's a tiny detail: The curve of his eyebrows, the shape of his nails, the flicker of humor in his eyes, the delicate nape of his neck, or those sexy veins that run down his arms. There are even times when it's a flaw of some kind: A gap in his teeth or a nose that's slightly crooked. Just about anything in a man can become the dwelling-place of your Thing.

We've seen that evolutionary biologists like to talk about men's bank accounts and résumés. Yet often it's a guy's uneven jaw line or some other "defect" that awakens your interest. And, luckily for you, this works the other way around as well so that it would be a mistake to work too hard at getting rid of the "imperfections" that bug you about yourself. It could be exactly these imperfections that make you appealing to potential lovers. I'm not saying that you shouldn't go to the dentist regularly, or that you shouldn't hit the gym once in a while. But you might as well give yourself a break about the quirky "shortcomings" that you think "ruin" you for the rest of the world. *You* might hate them, but they might actually be your biggest asset when it comes to attracting the right guy. If he fixates on them, it's because he senses that they provide an opening to something deeper in you that will resonate with a basic yearning of his. Similarly, whenever you're intrigued by some seemingly arbitrary detail in a man, chances are it's pointing you to something within him that's well worth exploring.

I've shown that desire is shockingly specific. You could meet a thousand hot and accomplished men and not be in any way moved by them. But then one day (usually a bad-hair day) you're getting a caramel Frappuccino at Starbucks and, voilà, there's your guy-Thing! Most times when we have an epiphany like this with a complete stranger, we walk away. We spot the ring on his finger or simply don't have the nerve to strike up a conversation. It's hard to walk up to a guy and say, "I think you might have my Thing," without coming off as a total lunatic. What sane guy is going to fall for a stalker-girl who corners him at the Starbucks counter? You could try picking up his iced latte, but that could lead to a situation where you have your first fight before you even know his name. So you let it go.

But sometimes luck is on your side and you have that spark with someone you have a good excuse to talk to. These are the moments when obsessions get kindled. They are the moments when you need to be vigilantly careful. But, if you understand the connection between desire and the Thing, they could also be moments that lead to something exceptional.

5

Your Thing-radar is highly sensitive. It almost always directs you to something significant, even when you're dealing with someone you've just met. I found one of my favorite guys like this, before a work meeting. He was standing outside the room where the meeting was going to be held, waiting for a colleague to unlock the door. I took one look at him and knew instantly that the two of us would hit it off. He was cute, but not cute enough to mow me down with sheer good looks. I honestly didn't know what drew me. Yet I knew right away that he definitely had the Thing. When we got to know each other better, it turned out that he was hopelessly hung up on his ex so that pursuing a romantic relationship wasn't an option. But this didn't change the fact that we did hit it off. And that the more time I spent with him, the more I liked him. My instinct has been dead-on. In that initial split-second, I had spotted the potential for a special connection.

There are often complications that keep us from exploring a connection like this. For instance, if the man we feel tantalized by is already attached, we may need to pull back forcefully. This is how we sometimes end up having entirely superficial relationships with the very men we are most compelled by. However, when everything else clicks into place, this kind of an intuitive bond can steer us to relationships that, quite literally, have the power to change our destiny. Such relationships are more fulfilling than a dozen ordinary ones combined. Even when they end badly, we may continue to feel their power years, even decades, after we've lost them. It's not that we necessarily think of them all the time. But when we do, there's a special quality to our reminiscences. It's as if the pragmatic texture of our daily lives was suddenly perforated by a sudden flash that belongs to some otherworldly domain. There's not much about life that's more stirring than this flash. This is why it's essential to know what kind of fire you're playing with when you're playing with your Thing (so to speak).

A man who conjures up your Thing for you also triggers your deepest vulnerability. We've learned that the Thing relates to amorphous sentiments of incompleteness, deprivation, helplessness, and inadequacy; it connects us to a loss that we cannot name. This unnameability makes our loss all the more grueling to cope with. It's hard to mourn something we cannot specify. Sigmund Freud had this in mind when he distinguished between two kinds of mourning. The first is the normal sorrow we experience when someone dies or we lose some beloved object or person. If what we have lost is unusually important to us, we may mourn for a very long time. However, at some point in the process we start to gradually dig our way out of our sadness. And, eventually, we'll be able to shift our attention to new objects and people; we'll we able to love again (more on this in Chapter 10). The second kind of mourning, in contrast, never quite comes to an end. We stay forever fixated on our loss. Freud speculated that this kind of endless mourning is more likely to occur when we are not exactly sure what it is that we have lost. He called this variety of mourning "melancholia."

The Thing relates to melancholia—to endless mourning. As a consequence, when a lover resurrects our Thing, he not only galvanizes our desire, but touches the melancholy essence of our being. We may not realize this at first because the intensity of our desire—and the euphoria that accompanies it—hides this melancholia from us. But, in due course, our melancholia is bound to surface. In Chapter 9, I'll talk more about the implications of this. For now, it's enough to recognize that the person who embodies the Thing for us—the person who promises us incomparable satisfaction—is also one who can hurt us more than anyone else. Precisely because he stands for the Thing, he can strike (often without meaning to) at the most defenseless, most melancholy reaches of our inner world. If the flipside of immense desire is immense woundability, it's because both our deepest joy and our deepest pain revolve around the Thing. This is why the guy who rouses our Thing from its stupor sometimes wields more power than he realizes.

Have you ever been infatuated with a man, unable to think of anything else? Or heartbroken to the point of not being able to function? If so, you can be sure that the man in question held out the promise of the Thing for you. Such lovers are precious beyond reckoning. And it won't take you long to tell the difference between a man who is just a regular date and one who has the potential to activate your Thing. By the time you think of it, the guy has most likely already done so. If not, odds are he never will.

Our culture judges this kind of desire to be treacherous, telling you that you're being reckless if you let first impressions dictate your romantic choices. I agree that it's good to have a healthy respect for the Thing's power to devastate you. Yet telling you to ignore this kind of attraction overlooks something crucial about how desire works. If there's anything "hard-wired" about people, it's not some biological male/female (hunter/prey) mentality, but rather the astonishing accuracy with which they locate their Thing in another person. If a subway car rarely yields a crop of men you want to have sex with, it's because love at first sight has little to do with the instinct to produce babies. It has to do with the distinctively *human* desire to recover a lost Paradise. This desire circles around your Thing and the guy who manages to stroke it in just the right way is the guy you can't get out of your mind.

This is yet another reason to drop all the relationship games you've been taught to play. The simple truth is that either a guy has your Thing, or he doesn't. Either you have his Thing, or you don't. Either you're his exception, or you're not. All the scheming in the world won't change this. You can't fake the Thing (even if you know how to fake that other thing—not that I recommend that either). A guy won't fall in love with you because you know how to dilate your pupils on demand. Rather, love happens when a guy's Thing meets your Thing. I don't mean this in an X-rated way. The X-rated things don't discriminate that much. They can make fireworks with pretty much anyone's thing. But the Things I'm talking about speak an inscrutable language that almost no one else in the world speaks. So when they meet each other, they're likely to feel jubilant.

Imagine living in the world for decades without meeting anyone who understands your language and then, one day, coming across someone who speaks it fluently. That's what falling in love feels like. And if you meet someone who can write poetry in your language, you can kiss your single life goodbye. Some people talk about soul mates. Or kindred spirits. These are lovely metaphors—mythological ways to describe something we don't fully understand. But we do now understand it a little better, don't we? We know that it's all about the Thing.

CHAPTER 8

....

Seeing the Extraordinary within the Ordinary

> **MYTH:** Seeing our lover through rose-tinted glasses prevents the growth of genuine intimacy.
>
> **FACT:** Ideals that illuminate hidden dimensions of our lover allow us to sustain love over time.

1

I've highlighted the problems that arise when love veers too close to idealization. We've seen that when a man turns a woman into a fantasy object, he erases her singularity. He ends up relating to an Olympia rather than a Clara. And he may even try to destroy her when he realizes that she can't match his ideals. Conversely, when we idealize a partner, we risk seeing only what we want to see. Although we usually mean well when we put a lover on a pedestal, our ideals can inflict a particular kind of violence: They can make our partner suspect that our adoration is aimed at an apparition that will dissipate with the first rays of dawn. Perhaps this is why falling in love with vampires is so popular these days. When the sun rises, a vampire conveniently retires to his coffin. His girlfriend never needs to look at him in the light of day. No wonder human guys can get a little jittery. It's hard to compete with a coffin-dweller who makes it his business to ravish unsuspecting virgins in soft candlelight.

Should we, then, stop idealizing those we love? By no means! Not only are ideals an unavoidable part of romance, but they help sustain desire over time. When our relationship loses its luster, it's usually because we've lost the capacity to idealize. We've lost the ability to raise our lover to the dignity of the Thing. The trick, therefore, is not to sidestep idealization. It's to learn to idealize in ways that respect the integrity of our lover.

Idealization is effortless in the beginning of a love affair. It's easy to feel that our lover is the greatest guy ever to walk the continent. We suspect he might be carved from a divine rock that fell to earth during a meteor shower. Even kryptonite won't diminish his power or tarnish his sparkle. The trouble is that our ideals take a beating every time our lover deviates from his superhuman persona. They chip away with every word or action that undermines our romanticized vision of him. It's amazing what a shapeless sweater or a bad tie can do to a relationship. And the more familiar we become with our partner, the more we tend to demote him from an extraordinary object to an ordinary one. The man who just a couple of months ago offered us a way out of the tedium of our everyday reality now becomes integral to that very tedium; he becomes part of the banal routine that romance was supposed to spice up.

Often enough, we have no idea why we no longer feel the thrill we initially felt. The death of desire is usually as enigmatic as its birth. If we don't know why we fall in love with a specific person, we also don't know why we fall out of love.

Nourishing desire over time requires that we stop viewing the ordinary and the extraordinary as two antithetical entities. It asks us to recognize that the man we love can be at once ordinary and extraordinary. This is what I meant when I said, in the previous chapter, that everyday dishes and Wentworth china are not mutually exclusive. If a relationship based solely on the Thing is bound to come tumbling down, one that denies the importance of the Thing will suppress what's most compelling about romance. On the one hand, if we choose to build a life with a steady partner, the bulk of that life will be composed of ordinary strands. On the other, if we lose track of the Thing, we condemn our relationship to a slow and torturous death. Our challenge, then, is to interlace the prosaic weave of the ordinary with some radiant filaments of the extraordinary. It's a bit like knitting a brown sweater with orange highlights. The extraordinary within the ordinary is the orange thread that winds in and out of the otherwise uniform brown background. The orange blends nicely with the brown. But it also stands out. It adds zest to the otherwise humdrum sweater.

Love should be zesty. It should be filled with ideals. Our lover should seem larger than life and inimitable, at least part of the time. He should stand out from the crowd. What's the point of being in love if we think that our guy is just like everyone else—if there's nothing to distinguish him from Mr. Average next door? We would be short-changing ourselves if we thought that there was nothing special about him. We would be cheating ourselves of joy if we believed that love is a matter of tolerating a person who has ceased to electrify us.

Sadly, this is how our culture often portrays "real" love. Real love, we're informed, is a matter of sticking it out even when we're stifling a yawn every time our partner opens his mouth to say something. Real love is about making sacrifices, learning to compromise, having sex even when we don't feel like it, and tending the fires of desire long after the embers have gone cold. Real love, in short, is a lot of work. We're supposed to grin and bear it even when it makes us feel as if we're toiling away in the bowels of an Alaskan gold mine.

I'm not so deluded as to think that couples should be able to sustain the first blush of passion over decades of married life. We all know that this is rarely possible. But I also don't think that marriage (or other long-term relationships) should feel like week seven of a two-month boot camp.

There are a few antidotes to this. Admitting that we don't know everything about our partner even when we know him very well is one of these. It allows us to continue to think of him as someone intriguing. Retaining an independent identity is also crucial. If we sacrifice our autonomy for the sake of our love—if we give everything up—we have nothing left to offer. The only way to guarantee that we have something to contribute in the long run is to make certain that we don't become a mere appendage of our partner; our purpose in life can't be to be his Plus One. Our most potent antidote, however, is our ideals. They have the power to arrest the dulling of romance. They can rescue us from not being able to tell the difference between our lover and the guy who delivers the newspaper in the morning. But we do need to know how to "use" them.

2

There are two ways to idealize. The first is to measure your lover against an external criterion. This could be something tangible: The guy in the Obsession ads, A-Rod, the lead singer of Coldplay, Denzel Washington, Johnny Depp, Jake Gyllenhaal, one of the Jonas brothers, Justin Timberlake, or Vampire Bill from *True Blood*. In a pinch, it could even be Tom Cruise. In a pinch. Or it could be something intangible: The vision of Mr. Right that you dreamt up when you were eight and stubbornly cherish even though there's rapidly accumulating evidence that you might have been an overly ambitious little girl.

By now you'll know that this is the "bad" way to idealize. The only thing it will accomplish is your perpetual disillusionment. Honestly, even the Johnny Depps of the world can't always live up to their image. Just think of Jude Law and the nanny. If Jude Law can disappoint you, you can be sure that your guy doesn't have a fighting chance of meeting your expectations. And he'll resent you for trying to make him. If he has any sense in him, he'll tell you that you're no Beyoncé either. And then he'll make a hasty exit. Good for him.

What's the "good" way to idealize, then? The good way is to find some appealing trait that your lover actually possesses and make a big deal of it. I don't mean that you should fixate on his bulging biceps and follow him around like a stray dog. I'm talking about developing some real appreciation for all the lovely and engaging attributes that your lover has. Sometimes this is a matter of highlighting a characteristic (say, intellect, kindness, or a great sense of humor) that is easily accessible right on the surface of his personality. But other times, it may be a matter of accenting some aspect of him that usually remains safely tucked away from the prying eyes of others. It may be a matter of breathing life into some repressed, neglected, overlooked, or underdeveloped quality that has lain dormant for far too long.

The easiest way to understand what this means, concretely, is to think about how we ourselves feel when we fall in love. We tend to feel intensely alive, connected to the most spontaneous layers of ourselves. In opening ourselves to a lover, we activate realms of our inner world that we may not visit very often. We invite him to emotional spaces that feel shy and timid. We drop the front that usually protects us from the unkind energies of our environment. This can be a huge relief. There's something uniquely comforting about the idea that there's a person in the world who loves us the way we are underneath our carapace.

Our carapace is necessary because it keeps out a lot of pain;

it ensures that we're not overwhelmed by what is wounding about the world. But it can also make us feel fake. It can make us feel numb and strangely out of touch with ourselves. As a result, there are few things that feel headier than being able to cast it off. There are few things that feel better than being able to reconnect with aspects of our being that have been forcefully suppressed. There is, in short, something enormously vitalizing about being able to trust that our lover will not recoil when we disclose the face beneath the mask.

The key to "good" idealization is to recognize that our partner feels the same way—that we have the power to rescue him from his phony self-presentations. We have the power to reanimate segments of his interiority that feel dead or frozen to him. We can, for instance, resurrect potentialities that may have been forcibly pushed aside by the relentless demands of making a living. That dream of being a journalist? It's probably still cowering in some corner of his consciousness while he spends his days wading through stacks of boring legal files. That vision of being a rock star? You can be sure it's lurking underneath the tranquil demeanor of the mild-mannered music teacher. That exquisite sensitivity to other people's moods? Or to the beauty of the surrounding world? Or to the delicate shape of dew drops on the window pane? It's a safe bet that it has been banished to some underground penitentiary by our society's demands on masculinity.

Whatever it is that is special about your lover but hidden from the world is your opening toward loving idealizations. You can make your lover feel effervescent by showing admiration for some of the things that lie in wait beneath the shield he upholds against a judgmental world. Often this is, quite simply, a matter of seeing what others can't see.

3

It's said that love is blind. I don't believe this. I think that love is actually unusually clear-sighted and perceptive. It allows us to discern dimensions of people that we normally overlook. It makes us keenly observant. Everything about our lover stirs our curiosity. Everything about him interests us. We become inquisitive, eager to explore. Our gaze is probing and pro-longed. We see things intensely, as if through a magnifying glass. When we are truly enchanted, it's hard for us to look away. And the more intimate we get with a lover, the more we are granted the privilege of seeing what others don't have access to. Love may rob us of all kinds of basic skills, such as the ability to stay focused at a work meeting. But it definitely does not strike us blind. Quite the contrary.

Under normal circumstances, we skim the surface of the world without paying much attention to its details. I often move around in such an automatic way that I don't fully regis-ter things I see on a daily basis. There have been times when I've realized that I've passed a building or a landmark every week for years without having really noticed it. Once I rented a fully furnished house for six months. The house was a jumble of knickknacks and ornaments. The owners had put a lot of effort into making it inviting. Whenever I took a break from writing, I wandered around the rooms and looked at the charming objects on display. There was a moment, five months into my rental, when I was taken by surprise by a sizable statue on the mantelpiece. This was in the room where I had sat writing every day. I was astounded that I could be so blind to what was right in front of me.

I guarantee that something like this would never happen with a guy I felt passionate about. I wouldn't go for five months without noticing the huge statue on the mantelpiece (to put it crudely). I trust the same is true for you. When we fall in love, we pay attention. Although some of what we see may be illusory—based on sand castles that we build in our imagination—much of what we unearth is valid. Often it's more valid than our absentminded everyday perception.

Plato recognized this a long time ago. He argued that the madness of love was comparable to the acumen of visionaries. And he thought that our worship of our lover's beauty was a stepping stone to transcendence. It was an indication that our soul was yearning for the company of the gods. The loveliness of the beloved was merely an earthly herald for the loveliness of divine truths. We don't need to believe in such truths to admit that Plato was onto something. The way we see when we are in love lifts us above the morass of our mundane concerns so that we are able to gain a glimpse of the most inspired realms of human life. We are able to find the extraordinary within the ordinary.

Let's be honest. We want the extraordinary. We want the elation of love. We even want the longing and the uncertainty.

Love not only adds flavor to our lives; it makes the rest of our activities meaningful. Our daily routine is filled with stress factors that bombard us from all sides. Our pace can be so crazy-making that it's difficult to hear our own thoughts. And we are often asked to perform repetitive tasks that muffle our senses and responses. Even something as simple as riding the bus or subway to and from work can, over time, become a tedious chore that consumes our energies. Our bodies—like our minds—can start to feel depleted. Falling in love feels so great in part because it counters this kind of weariness. It rejuvenates us, injecting a dose of exuberance into the every-day. It has a way of weaving even the most hardened of cynics into its web. Once caught, we don't want our freedom; we are willing prisoners. We are more than happy to look for the sublime kernel (our Thing) within our lover.

4

What we see in a person depends on how we look. We can either focus on what is extraordinary, even noble and mag-nificent. Or we can insist on the ordinary. Odds are that if we can no longer find anything extraordinary—anything worth idealizing—in our lover, we have stopped looking carefully. We have become complacent. We have allowed our mind's eye to dull. We may think that our level-headed practicality is the more mature, more realistic, approach. We may insist that we are finally seeing our lover as he "really is." But, actu-ally, being unable (or unwilling) to see the extraordinary is a sign that we have let our attention become superficial. We no longer see the exquisite statue on the mantelpiece. We have lost our spirit of generosity—the spirit that, in the beginning of a romance, empowers us to see what others don't see.

While it's easy to argue that this is just a part of the process that takes us from the initial surge of desire to a long-term commitment, one could also say that it represents an unfortunate lapse of imagination. If—as I have intimated—our lover is always to some degree opaque to us, he's by definition open to a range of interpretations; we can read him in a variety of ways. Aren't ideals, then, merely an indulgent way of seeing him? Aren't they a nonjudgmental means of forging togetherness?

Ideals that build on characteristics that our lover possesses are a way of releasing aspects of his being that he might not be able to free on his own. Again, it helps to think of how it feels when you yourself are on the receiving end of charitable idealizations. Particularly if you're someone who grew up with a lot of negative messages—as I did—you might need the loving words of idealizing partners to counteract the persistent residue of these messages. If you, for example, were told during your early years that you were never going to amount to anything, chances are you have internalized this assessment on such a deep level that it's difficult for you to believe anything else. Chances are you have a self-deprecating inner voice that tells you that you're bound to fail. I used to call this voice the monkey on my shoulder. It may take one or two genuinely generous lovers to neutralize it. Without such help, you might never find your way out of the maze of self-doubt that you've been trapped in.

The same applies to your lover. There are situations where your idealizations are, literally, life-changing. They offset the negative judgments that might have taken over his inner world. They offer a more encouraging interpretation of his potentialities. I'm not saying that you're responsible for his self-esteem, or that you need to become his therapist. I hope I've made it clear that we cannot rely on others to complete us or to conjure away our pain. But ideals, ultimately, are no less accurate than insults are. The truth lies somewhere in the middle. Someone who is used to hearing insults needs to hear some ideals in order to balance things out.

Remember Mr. Hyde from Chapter 1? He broke up with me by telling me that I wasn't beautiful enough for him. Had I been dating him when I was younger, I would have been crushed, for he reiterated an appraisal that my father had made repeatedly for the first couple of decades of my life. Fortunately for me, I had had a few boyfriends in between who had told me (equally repeatedly) that my father was mistaken. They had done everything in their power to knock that monkey off my shoulder. And they had succeeded. Theirs were the voices I heard when I listened to the break-up message. They provided a chorus of positive evaluations that crowded out the hurtful one I was receiving. It's hard to overestimate the value of something like this.

Those we love deserve to be approached with a bit of stardust and a pair of rose-tinted glasses. Seeing the extraordinary within our lover does not mean that we ignore his shortcomings. Or forgive him when he treats us badly. But it does mean that we take a benevolent view of all those things that make him distinctive. An important part of this is showing him that we see the best in him. At the same time, it's essential to let him know that it's okay to fall short of our ideals. The worst we could do would be to give him the impression that he's only lovable to the extent that he incarnates our Thing. We need to be able to convey that our ideals are meant to empower rather than to oppress.

In addition, we can never forget that these ideals are of our own making—that they do not represent the entire reality of our lover. They may not be any less truthful than a jaded and overly pragmatic lens. But they are not who our lover is either. They are merely one among many ways of understanding him. We cannot thus expect that he will always adhere to them. As much as it may please us to be dating a creature carved out of divine stone, we must also allow for the awkward fumblings of the mortal who shares our fridge and Netflix account. The mundane side of Superman's cape are Clark Kent's clumsy glasses. When we shun the latter, we lose the former.

Ideals must be used judiciously. When we expect our lover to stay faithful to our ideals, we rob him of his right to have flaws. If the positive face of idealization is to communicate to our lover that he is capable of more than he might believe, its negative face is to suggest that anything short of perfection will dishearten us. When we activate this negative face—when we imply that the cost of our lover's inability to live up to our ideals is the loss of our love—our ideals cease to be gifts of generosity and become, instead, tools of terror. They can only do the constructive work of revising our lover's self-perception as long as he knows that our love will survive their collapse. They can only enhance our relationship as long as they leave our lover plenty of space to be less than ideal.

When we idealize well, we manage to maintain an equilibrium between the ordinary and the extraordinary. We don't lose track of the ways in which our lover is entirely ordinary. We admit that he has habits and quirks that can be irksome. We recognize that he is prone to anxiety, worry, doubt, insecurity, and indecision in exactly the same way as we are. And we know that he is as weighted down by his past, as conflicted, as the next person. At the same time, we stay attuned to the various ways in which he remains extraordinary. After all, we wouldn't have fallen in love with him if he had not revealed some qualities worth admiring. There must have been something that made our pulse quicken. Over time, it may become difficult to access these special qualities. But this doesn't mean that they have ceased to exist. Or that we were mistaken in once seeing them.

5

When love ends badly, we often try to convince ourselves that the extraordinary qualities we saw in our ex were completely erroneous. Sometimes this is true. There are times when we are fooled by a dazzling surface that hides a problematic core. Many abusive men start out as charismatic and considerate lovers. They may in fact be more charismatic and considerate than the average nice guy because, on some level, they're aware that they have a problem. They may be trying to keep the nasty side of themselves from surfacing by acting the part of the perfect boyfriend.

This was the case with Mr. Hyde. He was smart enough to know that he had a tendency to hurt the women he was with. And, because he was not all evil, he tried his best to keep this from happening. He was so magnificent in the initial stages of the relationship that when the reversal happened, I was taken completely by surprise. The turnaround was so dramatic that I couldn't make any sense of it. I kept thinking that it was a temporary blip that would pass as suddenly as it had appeared—that he was just stressed out at work or otherwise under pressure. And, as is common in such situations, I kept thinking that there was something I could do to return things back to "normal." I now know that "normal" for this man is what he became rather than what he at first was. As much as he might want to change his behavior, he can't—not without professional help.

So, absolutely, there are times when our ideals mislead us. But often when we retroactively downgrade our past lover from the realm of the extraordinary to the realm of the entirely ordinary, we are doing so out of grief or anger. We may need to do so in order to endure the pain of the breakup. But it's also likely that we're being a little unfair to our ex—that, in our misery, we're choosing to emphasize the negative over the positive. And we're also doubting our own prior opinion. We're trying to convince ourselves that our original assessment was mistaken—that there was nothing unique about our lover to begin with. Our culture encourages this view by telling us that love clouds our judgment. I think, though, that the elevated image we hold of our lovers is rarely entirely wrong. It's just that the condemning post-breakup appraisal obliterates it so effectively that we no longer see it.

It may be understandable (even if it is not excusable) that we are sometimes driven to reduce our ex to his worst qualities after a breakup. But let's not do that to the lover we're still with. Let's not insist that there's nothing in him worth venerating. Let's in fact actively look for ways to see what is luminous about him. If our powers of perception are a little dusty, let's brush ourselves off. If the mirror we hold up to our lover is a little lackluster, let's polish it up. There's a lot about life that's dreary and unexciting. Let's not insist that our lover join the club of all the other boring things that vie for dominance in our daily existence. Let's make sure that we don't drown out what is captivating and incomparable about him in the name of some matter-of-fact realism. Whatever quality it is that first scintillated us about him is most likely still within him. One of our foremost tasks in romance is to keep alive our ability to notice it.

True love must survive the defeat of ideals. But it must also survive the overwhelming pressure of overfamiliarity. It must fend off the triteness that quietly nibbles at the edges of romance, gradually turning it into just another facet of the commonplace. Those who manage to sustain passion over time know how to arrest the steady advance of this triteness. They know how to insert ideals into the composition of their lives. They understand that their loved ones are not either ordinary or extraordinary, but both at once.

Love that does not tolerate the breakdown of ideals is too stingy. But so is love that refuses to idealize. Let's not kid ourselves. When we fall in love, we long for something bigger and better than the everyday. We yearn to be transported to a magical domain that makes up for some of the insipidness of our ordinary existence. The worst we could do would be to bury this yearning under some bland vision of down-to-earth pragmatism. The worst we could do would be to demote our lover from a sublime object to a meaningless bauble.

CHAPTER 9

....

Breaking the Patterns of Pain

> **MYTH:** Lovers who trigger our unconscious conflicts should be avoided at all costs.
>
> **FACT:** Lovers who awaken our conflicts can sometimes usher us to higher levels of maturity and self-understanding.

1

I've argued that sparks fly when your Thing meets a guy's Thing. This is the good news. The bad news is that falling in love brings together two creatures who both have a highly idiosyncratic unconscious. The unconscious is the little devil within us that derails our rational plans. Astrologers like to say that it's Mercury retrograde that makes our lives go haywire so that we lose things, miss appointments, forget our mother's birthday, and sleep with our ex when we really should know better. But I'm telling you it's the unconscious.

Usually, the only time we're aware of this little devil is when we make one of those awkward Freudian slips, or wake up from a vivid dream. Freud specified that dreams are the "highway to the unconscious." Mine must be an arid waste-land, for the only dream I'm able to come up with regularly is one where I dial a phone number over and again, only to always make a mistake in one of the last digits. I don't know who I'm trying to call. Or what the burning issue is. All I know is that I never get through—and it's always my own slip-up that causes the disconnect. If I could just once punch those ten numbers correctly, I'm sure all my problems would immediately solve themselves.

Let's do a little thought experiment to understand why your love life can sometimes begin to resemble this dream. Imagine you're on vacation in Europe. You board a train in Geneva, Switzerland, that's supposed to take you to Rome. But you arrive in Paris instead. You're puzzled. It's not that you don't like Paris. But you really had your heart set on Rome. So you go back to Geneva, hoping to catch the next train to Rome. But here's what happens. You keep boarding the Rome-bound train. And you keep arriving in Paris. Each time you step onto the platform, you're greeted by a flock of snotty Parisian pigeons.

After a while, you start to get pretty frustrated. You've already been to Paris a dozen times. You've seen the *Mona Lisa* (and wasn't *that* a disappointment?). You've paid your respects to the saints of Notre Dame. You've toured the Latin Quarter until you can't stand the sight of yet another tortured artist (or American tourist). And you've bought an overpriced *demi* on the Champs-Élysées so many times that you've burned a hole in your pocket. You've heard that Rome is full of hot Italian guys and you're eager to get there. In fact, the more Rome eludes you, the more desperate you are to reach it. So you give it one last try. You plan your itinerary with extra care. You pore over maps of Western Europe to memorize all the train stations between Geneva and Rome. You fly in a friend from San Francisco who is fluent in French, German, and Italian to buy your ticket for you (even though the sales agents at the Geneva train station speak better English than you do). You want to make absolutely sure that when you get off that train, it's the walls of the Vatican rather than the Arc de Triomphe that you set your eyes on.

Well, guess what? When you get off the train, one of those Parisian pigeons poops all over your Gucci luggage. *That's the unconscious for you.* You sit down on the filthy platform of Gare de Lyon and sob. Obviously, there's something seriously wrong with you. As soon as you return to New York, you find yourself a shrink who reminds you of your father. Five years—and fifty thousand dollars—later, you have one of those eureka moments: It's all because your father refused to buy you an ice cream cone at Grand Central Station when you were three!

Most of us never figure out the root cause of our neuroses. But we all have them. And, typically, our neuroses entail some sort of repetition. Let's say you've had three relationships in a row where the guy you were dating made you feel like item 27 on his to-do list (okay, item 36 in one case). You told each of these guys that you needed them to make you a priority in their lives. You were polite about it, utilizing the negotiation skills recommended by Dr. Phil. Each time, your boyfriend told you that he would make time for you "from now on." But, each time, his good intentions fell apart within days so that you once again felt yourself sliding down that infernal list until you were wedged somewhere between "pick up dry-cleaning" and "call that guy—was his name Jason?—I met in Aspen two years ago."

After you break up with the last of these losers, you resolve to make sure that this will never ever happen again. On every new date, you interrogate your prospect about how he spends his time and how important romance is to him. You finally find a guy you know will give you the attention you deserve. He's an ex-investment banker who retired at thirty-five after making a killing on the stock market. He only works one day a month. He hates parties and only has two friends. He has consulted every spiritual leader from Deepak Chopra to Eckhart Tolle so he's all about connecting with his soul mate. And he has spent a couple of years in India studying the secrets of Tantric sex. What could possibly go wrong?

Nothing, for a while. You're the center of his life. You've never felt so loved and appreciated. Ten months pass. You're blissfully happy. Then, one day, your guy announces that he wants to write a book about Tantric sex. He disappears into his study. You barely see him for three months. And when you do, he's exhausted and cranky. He has turned into a moody *artiste* who prefers to brood over his scotch rather than to talk to you. And, no, he's definitely not in the mood for sex. All that writing about it has given him a pounding headache. You're mystified. How could this happen? You were so careful. You hand-picked this guy because he was the exact opposite of all the other guys who made you feel neglected. You definitely didn't see *this* coming!

2

We rarely do. That's how unconscious repetition works. It gets us every time. Freud had a name for this: The repetition compulsion. He explained that when we are in the grip of this compulsion, we feel as if our fates were determined by some evil power outside of us—by something a bit like the wizard behind the curtain in *The Wizard of Oz*. And, after a while, the incessant repetition of the same tired plotlines makes us feel like hamsters on a wheel, as if we were running around in circles without ever getting anywhere.

Freud also warned us that the repetition compulsion is nowhere as powerful as in the realm of romance. This is because falling in love activates deep-seated patterns of relating that we learned early on, through our relationship with our parents (or other caretakers). It mobilizes parts of our psyches that are so foundational that they feel unshakable. These are default patterns of love that have become so well established that we never pause to think about them. The most elementary layers of our personality have formed around them. As a result, we enact them mechanically, without questioning their efficacy. Yet there's no guarantee that they're good for us.

If you grew up in a warm and loving family, chances are that you've internalized some helpful patterns of relating. By this I don't mean that you're damaged unless you had a model family with two angelic parents who never bickered and never said a cross word to you. For most of us, *The Waltons* and *Little House on the Prairie* are the closest we ever got to perfect family idyll. Fortunately, it doesn't matter how many parents you had, how saintly or unsaintly they were, how much money they made, or how many arguments you overheard. What matters is what you learned about your own worth and about relating.

As children, our hunger for love is so immense that no parents, however adoring, can ever fully meet it. They will always disappoint us in one way or another. A big part of growing up is learning to tolerate the fact that our needs are not always met. This won't damage our self-esteem or relationship skills. But being treated badly will. Those who had devoted families are likely to have an easier time with romance than those who were neglected, abused, or trampled upon.

The way we are cared for when we are young gives us a blueprint for relating. It teaches us how to love and be loved. And it equips us with a highly specific set of expectations. When we form relationships later in life, a lot depends on these expectations. A lot depends on the kinds of emotional scenarios we're willing to accept. If I anticipate love and respect, my chances of attracting these are pretty good. If I predict frustration and disillusionment, I'm likely to find these. This is what people mean when they talk about self-fulfilling prophesies. The problem is that such prophesies are often unconscious, so that we are not fully aware of them. What we consciously think about romance may be very different from what our unconscious "thinks." For example, even when we consciously tell ourselves that we're lovable, our unconscious may insist that we're not.

Unfortunately, it's our unconscious beliefs that tend to determine how we interact with those we love. They organize our love lives around certain kinds of relational possibilities while closing off others. In a sense, we are only able to attain what we can, unconsciously, envision. So, if our unconscious can't picture a mutually loving relationship, odds are we'll also find it hard to achieve one. Bad romances, in contrast, are easy to come by because bad unconscious scripts are as common as Slovenians in downtown Ljubljana.

No matter how many new experiences we accumulate, the scripts of love we internalized as children stay etched within our psyches. For instance, if we had a rejecting and overly critical father, we might find that we often, without intending to, end up dating rejecting and overly critical men. Or, if we had an overbearing mother, we might find ourselves feeling smothered in our relationships. To return to my train simile, our desire is like a train that's set to run the same course indefinitely. We can't change this course without talking to Central Command (the unconscious). And we can't derail the train without causing major havoc. The train is scheduled to stop at predesignated stations along the way. These stations symbolize our worst hang-ups and fixations. They carry names such as "Rejection," "Frustration," "Desolation," "Disenchantment," and "Bitter Disappointment." As much as we would like to avoid them, the train we're on stops at them without fail. Which is why we sometimes end up in Paris when we want to go to Rome.

3

Is there a point to the repetition? What causes the train to stop at these tear-soaked stations? The answer is a lot more interesting than you might expect. It's not that folks who repeat agonizing patterns are caught up in a masochistic attempt to hurt themselves. Even if there's some twisted pleasure in the pain they experience, their end game is bigger. They're desperately trying to overcome a hurtful emotional blueprint. They entertain the hope that repetition will lead to resolution.

When you think about it, this is not that crazy. If you want to become a world-class swimmer, you can't just watch videos of Michael Phelps. You'll need to put in a lot of hours in the pool. If you want to become an expert in nineteenth-century English literature, you'll need to read a lot of Charles Dickens, Thomas Hardy, George Eliot, and Jane Austen. If you want to become the next Yo-Yo Ma, you'll need to spend a lot of time at the cello. And if you dream of becoming a forensic pathologist, you'll need to hit those science books. So...it's not that idiotic to think that if you want to become better at relating, you'll need to put yourself in painful relationship dilemmas until you learn your lesson.

Each of us has been traumatized in one way or another. The depth of our injuries varies, but there's no human psyche that has completely escaped pain. And our wounds mold our character so that, in a certain sense, who we are has a lot to do with how we have been hurt. Each eccentric pattern of pain leads to an eccentric mode of dwelling in the world. What's so heartbreaking about the repetition compulsion is that it aims to transcend pain even as it ends up inflicting more of it. It seeks to right the wrongs of the past by "mastering" a traumatic pattern. We are driven to a repetition because, on a deep level, we believe that *this time* things will be different—that we'll finally be able to emerge unscathed from a relational dynamic that has wounded us before. We believe that repeating an excruciating scenario will allow us to conquer those aspects of our history that hold us down. So it's likely that if you frequently find yourself item 27 on your boyfriend's to-do list, you're trying, in a roundabout way, to deal with deep-rooted feelings of never being good enough for those who are supposed to love you.

Repetition is a sign that you're trying to work through an unresolved issue. Before you start scolding yourself for your latest romantic misstep, it may be useful to ask yourself what you might have unconsciously sought to accomplish through that misstep. What is the work your soul is seeking to do when it obstinately gets caught up in the same heartrending scenario? What wound are you attempting to heal?

We've seen that our self-help culture tells us that love should be clear-cut and transparent. Liz Tuccillo, for instance, urges women to make the following vow about their future relationships: "No more murky, no more gray, no more unidentified, and no more undeclared." This is a valiant sentiment. But it disregards the fact that romance is designed to stir the waters of the unconscious. Not only is love, by definition, gray, but our responses to it are almost inevitably murky. Instead of thinking of this as a failure, it might help to acknowledge that the murkier things get, the closer we are to catching the devil that keeps throwing a monkey wrench into our relationships.

The biggest mistake we could make with the repetition compulsion would be to deny its power. Our biggest mistake would be to pretend that we can rationally "decide" to do love differently—that we have the ability to make our relationships black and white rather than murky. We'll gain a lot more if we admit that there's likely to be a point in every relationship when repetition gets the better of us.

If we flee from a lover to escape our repetition compulsion, we're likely to enact it just as strongly with our next lover. This doesn't mean that we should always stick with the first of these lovers. We may have good reasons for leaving him. But it's important to understand that there's no way to build an intimate relationship without rousing the dormant ghosts of the past. And the more these ghosts have been suppressed, the hungrier they are. When our relationship develops, all of our buried sorrow, sadness, longing, and anger float to the surface, suddenly hankering for attention. As does the melancholia I talked about in Chapter 7. The harmony of new love keeps these sentiments at bay for a time. But sooner or later, they will clamor for notice. At that junction, we have a choice. We can either bravely face our ghosts by entering into some sort of a negotiation with them, or we can back away from the relationship that's awakening them. If we expect our relationships to be unambiguous, we're likely to do the latter. But this may not always be the right choice.

I'm usually the first to tell friends to bail out of wounding romantic entanglements. But when it comes to the repetition compulsion, I would recommend some patience. I would recommend some lenience both with ourselves and our lovers. There's no relationship that's entirely free of crises and obstacles. Most of us have issues that get to us. And our unconscious is an expert at choosing men who know how to trigger these issues. The same goes for our lovers. When we welcome a man into our lives, we also extend an invitation to his issues. We extend an invitation to all the personal history that has made him who he is today. We summon the ghosts of his past into the present—right into the folds of our relationship. This is always a little dangerous. And when two people's issues collide, the result can be downright explosive.

When two lovers provoke each others' hungry ghosts, things can get murky very fast. It's helpful, then, to remember that when our lovers push our buttons, they usually do so unintentionally. There have probably been times when you yourself have accidentally said or done something that upset your partner. You didn't mean to. And, most likely, neither did your partner when he did or said something that hurt you. It's almost impossible to find a long-term relationship that hasn't endured its share of acting out. Couples who stay together either find a way to work through their issues, or reconcile themselves to being miserable. The rest of us go through cycles of trial and error where we strive to get the better of a situation we can't quite control. When we end a romance with someone, it's often because we couldn't find a way out of the repetition compulsion—either our own or that of our partner. We were unable to break the patterns of pain. So we broke up instead.

4

What makes it doubly difficult to surmount the repetition compulsion is that the line between repetition and emotional violence is sometimes quite blurry. I just said that people are usually not intentionally cruel. *Usually.* There are times when they are. This is when heading for the exit is a good idea. But sometimes it takes a long time to determine whether you're in pain because you're being tormented by a bunch of famished ghosts, or because your boyfriend is acting like an unmitigated jerk.

Take my friend Amanda and her boyfriend Chris. Chris is funny and romantic. In many ways, he's the best partner Amanda has ever had. But he's also bossy. He criticizes her over the smallest things, such as leaving the pepper shaker on the kitchen counter after dinner. If you're starting to have visions of Julia Roberts in *Sleeping with the Enemy*, you're not far off. Chris doesn't beat Amanda up. But he makes her cry on a daily basis. When she does, he doesn't apologize or try to comfort her. Instead, he tells her—in the overly patient voice that parents sometimes use with disobedient children—that she's overreacting. He pushes the blame for their problematic dynamic onto her, implying that she's drowning in a misery of her own making. Not surprisingly, this only makes her more upset.

Amanda may have issues with her self-esteem and capacity to stand up for herself. But Chris clearly has plenty of issues of his own. And he keeps passing the buck to Amanda because he's not willing to do the work of figuring out how these issues are damaging their relationship. Why is he so controlling and critical? Why does it bother him so much to find the pepper shaker on the kitchen counter? And why does he deny Amanda's right to feel hurt? He thwarts Amanda's attempts to express her feelings by implying that she shouldn't be having them in the first place. The underlying message of his reactions is that if she were less needy or hysterical, she wouldn't be so distressed. Even though it's his own behavior that's generating much of the tension between them, he finds a way to make it all about her.

Shifting the blame is, unfortunately, a common technique of emotional manipulation. Although both men and women are capable of it, there are cultural reasons for why women are more often on the receiving end of it. To the extent that a woman has been taught to be meek and receptive (soft and feminine), she's vulnerable to any guy who chooses to turn the tables on her. A guy who resorts to this strategy manages to convince you that, no matter how abusively he behaves, your bad feelings are your own fault. If you feel wounded, it's because you're overly sensitive. If you're crying, you're overly emotional. If you want to talk things through, you're overly analytical. If you ask him to change the way he treats you, you're overly demanding. This is a convenient way for a man to evade responsibility for his behavior. It's a way to absolve himself of any emotional accountability to you. According to his reasoning, your suffering is your own doing. If you react badly to something he says or does, that's your problem, isn't it?

When I lived on Maui—the New Age capital of the world (populated by refugees from the mainland who think that California is too mainstream for them)—I saw how even New Age rhetoric could be used against women in this way. A lot of New Age philosophies emphasize that we're all responsible for our own happiness. In principle, this is a great idea. Obviously I can't hold anyone else responsible for my well-being. But if you want to exploit this idea, nothing is easier. You can say and do the most provoking things conceivable without having to worry about their impact on others. If your lover's feelings are always her own responsibility, there's no need to monitor your words and actions.

I had one Maui man tell me that my anger about him having lied to my face (which I discovered accidentally) was "unenlightened." A more spiritually evolved person, he stressed, wouldn't get so offended. She would "own" her anger by letting it flow through her. "It's all about your attitude," he volunteered. I couldn't believe my ears. This guy blatantly betrayed my trust. And then he tried to convince me that my anger about it was some sort of a spiritual failure! This made my blood boil even more than his duplicity. I realized that he gets away with his New Age "line" all the time. He's the quintessential wolf in a sheep's clothing—the reason *Little Red Riding Hood* became an international bestseller.

This was an isolated incident. And I was so not the woman to fall for it. I might have even waved my Harvard degree under his nose and said: "See—*not stupid!*" But I can well imagine sliding into such a dynamic gradually. This is what happened to Amanda. When she first started dating Chris, he was charming and attentive. He showered her with little romantic gestures that made her feel wonderful. It was much later—when Amanda was already emotionally invested— that he began to act cruelly. By the time the pepper shaker became a problem, she was so immersed in the relationship that it was hard for her to detach herself. Like many women in similar circumstances, she started to tiptoe around Chris, skulking around like a stray cat so as not to call attention to herself. She thought that the smaller she made herself, the less likely he was to notice and disparage her. She, in short, became apologetic about the simple fact of taking up space in the world. And she started to believe that she really was too needy and hysterical—that there was something pathological about her yearning for basic human kindness.

This degree of anxiety will grind down even the strongest of women. It will ruin your self-esteem and make you doubt your sanity. If a guy criticizes you constantly and then tells you that you don't have the right to be upset, chances are you won't get too far if you try to work through your repetition compulsions with him. So, the first step in being able to break a painful romantic pattern is to determine whether your guy is willing to meet you halfway.

In Chapter 6, I stressed that it's pointless to run after men who aren't that thrilled about being with you. Likewise, it's a waste of your energies to seek to overcome repetitions with a man who can't accept responsibility for his share of the undertaking. Some lovers are worth the investment. Others are not. When you're dealing with an emotional thug, you'll find yourself trying to anticipate his every mood just to keep yourself safe. But when you're dealing with a guy who has enough sweetness and backbone to be able to enter into the kind of joint venture that the process of dissolving outdated relational patterns requires, you're in luck. You are standing at the threshold of a tremendous opportunity.

Being able to face the ghosts of your past in the context of a loving relationship offers you a rare chance to reinvent your life. This is why murkiness is sometimes better than clarity. It invites you to descend a creaky ladder into the dim cellar of your unconscious. It insists that you shine a flashlight at how your past is dictating your present.

Why is it, for example, that you can't stand it when your lover needs space? What is it about his craving for privacy that threatens you? If you can find some answers, you may be able to recondition your responses. And if you find a way to effectively communicate your answers to your partner, he may be able to adjust his behavior so as to accommodate your fears. This doesn't mean that his need for space will diminish, but he may be able to soften its impact on you by assuring you that it has nothing to do with you. He may even tell you that his longing for periods of aloneness is not meant to distance him from you, but rather to enable him to love you better. Some people need solitude to love well; they need time for themselves in order to be able to spend quality time with you. It's hard to know something like this about another person unless you ask him about it. Your repetition compulsion is meant to nudge you to do so. It's meant to prod you into deeper levels of intimacy.

5

When the personal history of one individual meets the personal history of another individual, there is bound to be some fear and trembling. There is bound to be emotional reorganization. But this can be productive. Moments when painful patterns arise in a relationship can become important occasions for growth. Sure, they cause seismic shifts. They risk toppling the house of cards you've so carefully assembled. They create fissures in the polished edifice of your identity. Yet this disorder can have fruitful consequences. It can remobilize sediments of your interiority that have become too stubborn, too habitual. It can even liquidate redundant parts of your being, in much the same way as a vigorous spring cleaning prompts you to finally get rid of the junk in your attic. Precisely because it destabilizes the habitual boundaries of your life, it can usher you to a higher level of maturity and self-reflexivity.

Although it would be easier if love was always smooth and effortless, relationship difficulties oblige you to confront the most persistent sticking points of your existence. If you can work through such sticking points, you'll access new sources of energy; you'll discover previously unimaginable forms of loving and living. You might even, finally, get to Rome.

In a perverse way, the repetition compulsion is correct when it insists that practice makes you perfect. If you never meet a lover who is able to activate your most archaic patterns, you might never get a chance to break these patterns; you might never get an opportunity to learn the lessons you're meant to learn. This is something to keep in mind the next time someone advises you to find a man who is free of conflicts.

In our pragmatic self-help culture, we're often told that "difficult" men are trouble. But I would say that difficult men are trouble only if they're abusive. If they're byzantine in a benign way, they might actually be better at forcing us to evolve than less complicated men. I'm not saying that you should date Mr. Insane, Mr. Liar, Mr. Compulsive-Cheater, or Mr. Can-Never-Commit. But what's so wrong with Mr. Feeling-a-Little-Torn or Mr. Need-Time-to-Figure-Things-Out? Haven't we all been there at some point in our lives? How many of us can truthfully say that we come with a clean slate? Or that we have never been confused in a relationship? Why, then, not show a little generosity with men's messy emotions and passions? Sometimes it's the lover who challenges you the most who is also most deserving of your efforts.

It's essential to realize, though, that breaking counterproductive patterns is not something we ever fully accomplish. It can always only be an imperfect (and ongoing) process. There may even be times when we slide backward. That's okay. The point is not to conquer the unconscious. The point, rather, is to become more aware of how it motivates our behavior. The point is to identify the part we unconsciously play in the crafting of our emotional destiny.

Among other things, this enables us to take responsibility for the ways in which our words and actions impact the lives of others. I don't agree with those who claim that everyone is fully (and exclusively) responsible for his or her own feelings. I believe that we are radically responsible for the welfare of those close to us. By this I don't mean that it's our job to secure their happiness. But I do think that we are responsible for how our words and actions make them feel. As adults, we are able to anticipate the reactions of others. If I lie to my lover, cheat on him, say cutting things to him, or criticize him without cause, I know I'm likely to wound him. Pretending otherwise is dishonest. There may be times when I guess badly—when I can't accurately predict his responses. As I already suggested, all of us slip occasionally so that we end up hurting those we love without meaning to. But, in most cases, feigning ignorance about the likely impact of our behavior is a pretext for evading accountability.

The more we understand our repetition compulsion, the easier it is for us to catch ourselves when we're in danger of saying or doing something hurtful. When the compulsion runs our lives without our permission, it causes us to act defensively—from a place of emotional rigidity; we end up reacting automatically, without thinking. In contrast, when we start to pay attention to our patterns, we gain the power to intervene. We come to recognize that our customary ways of interacting with our loved ones are merely one option among others. As a consequence, we become capable of more flexible responses. We get to resketch the basic outline of our relationships.

This is why a "complicated" alliance might sometimes be good for us. While it may be tempting to think that there's a lover out there who will allow us to sidestep our issues completely, this is unlikely. Obviously, we don't want to stay with a guy who is wearing us down with emotional violence. But if our lover is open and caring, it would be a mistake to flee from him just because he raises the curiosity of our inner ghosts. Like the designated driver on a party night, he is chosen for this job for a reason. He deserves our gratitude. If we're fortunate, he holds in his hand an engraved invitation to a more rewarding future.

CHAPTER 10

....

A Love Failure Is Not
a Life Failure

> **MYTH:** The failures of love are a deviation from
> its mission—which is to make us happy.
>
> **FACT:** Some of our most meaningful
> love affairs are those that fail.

1

We have seen that love celebrates the extraordinary within the ordinary. This, however, should not be confused with the idea that it leads to everlasting happiness. We're culturally conditioned to think that it should. Yet happiness is rarely the result of love. To be sure, there are happy marriages and happy long-term relationships. But often those who have been lucky enough to find these happy unions have had to go through a whole slew of painful ones first. Their happy relationship might be the seventh relationship they have tried. So the odds are 1 in 7. Or 1 in 16. Or, if you're like my friend Philip, 1 in 867. Even if the odds were 1 in 5, they wouldn't be great odds. And then there's the fact that many happy marriages and relationships will, over time, become unhappy.

Half of married Americans eventually get a divorce, and far more relationships end in a breakup than a happily-ever-after. And this doesn't take into account the folks who stay in unhappy marriages and relationships. So I'm thinking that love might actually be one of the least effective ways of gaining happiness.

The catch-22 of love is that it has the power to make us happier than pretty much anything else in the world, but whenever we step into it, we risk unfathomable unhappiness. Scholars who study ethics like to talk about two scenarios that Immanuel Kant introduced back in the eighteenth century. The first involves a man who is granted the following choice: Give false testimony (that will condemn an innocent man to death) or be hanged. Kant tells us that the ethical thing to do would be to be hanged: It would be wrong to send an innocent man to the gallows. The second scenario involves a man who is given a slightly different choice: Abstain from sleeping with a lady (presumably the love of your life) or be hanged. Kant tells us that only a fool would sleep with the lady—that you would have to be a total idiot to sacrifice your whole life for the sake of one night with a beautiful woman.

Kant may not have been a great romantic, but he definitely has a point. Yet, when it comes to love, most of us arguably behave like a man who chooses to sleep with a lady even though he knows that he might be hanged in the morning. We don't have much of a choice, do we?

Every time we risk our hearts, the chance of getting hanged (metaphorically speaking) is much higher than the chance of happiness. One would think that with all the evolutionary progress of the last four million years, humans would have figured out by now that there's only the faintest of connections between love and well-being. Many of us come to this realization periodically. After a bad breakup, we might swear off love for a while. But love is tenacious. It has powerful potions that are hard to resist. And so most of us succumb to its charms sooner or later.

I know one guy who tried to "solve" the catch-22 of love by sleeping with as many women as possible without forming any emotional bonds. This is one way to go about it. It's a good alternative to tracking down the closest monastery and signing up for a life of solitary contemplation. But here's what happened. This guy went merrily from woman to woman until, one day, he realized that he was head-over-heels for a woman who wouldn't date him because he was such a notorious womanizer. His strategy backfired big time. Once again, he found himself in love and miserable.

We all know that there's a good reason fairy tales end when the hero and the heroine find a way to overcome all the obstacles stacked against them and live happily ever after. We know that what happens after the moment the princess kisses the frog doesn't make for good entertainment because it may well turn out that the frog is, really, just a frog. Yet it's difficult not to be seduced by fairy-tale endings. Like a mild day in the middle of a Minnesota winter, happiness is one of those things that's almost impossible not to want. *We cannot not want it.* I don't know about you, but I've never met a person whose mission in life was to be wretchedly unhappy. Some of us end up that way anyway. But it's usually not a goal that we pursue consciously. This being the case, it's almost miraculous that so many of us insist on falling in love. And it's even more stunning that some of us keep doing it over and again, even after we have been burned more times than we care to admit.

2

Is there something wrong with us then? Are we really the idiots that the Kantian analogy would make us out to be? I don't think so. I think that in the most secret recesses of our being, we know that love has aims that are loftier than happiness.

Don't get me wrong. I'm not saying that happiness is not worth the fight. Or that there's something banal about it. I'm not one of those people who think that there's nobility to be had from pain and suffering. It's just that when it comes to the complexity of human emotions, happiness might be overrated. Europeans know this, which is why they poke fun at the all-American pursuit of happiness (even as they secretly envy it). First of all, we are only able to register happiness as happiness because it's merely one among an array of feelings: If we were consistently happy, we would quickly lose our ability to appreciate it, or even to recognize it. More importantly, a steady stream of happiness would rob us of a large assortment of emotions that are necessary for the ripening of our character.

Although feelings of all shape and caliber are valuable for the task of crafting a complex character, happiness may be one of the least useful. This is because it fixes us into a spot. Whenever we feel content, we want things to stay exactly as they are; we don't want to undermine our happiness by changing anything. This is fine as long as we are willing to accept stagnation as the status quo of our lives. But if we are interested in growth, this status quo needs to be shaken once in a while. This is where the failures of love come in handy. A romantic malfunction asks us to rethink our lives from top to bottom. The emotional turmoil it generates forces us to reconsider things that we have come to take for granted. It invites us to explore edges of our emotional universe that might otherwise escape our attention.

Under normal conditions, it's hard to stay focused on what is most important to us. We get distracted in a million different ways. Our various responsibilities prod us in countless directions. We can get so caught up in the practical demands of living that we lose sight of our deepest passions; we lose track of the larger goals and ambitions that give meaning to our lives. A romantic disappointment puts an end to all of this. It paralyzes us so that we cannot go on with our usual concerns. We may even fall behind at work or with other personal obligations. Our culture tells us that the best thing to do in such circumstances is to get back on our feet as quickly as possible. It implies that there's something self-indulgent about wallowing in our misery and obsessing about the details of who did what and what went wrong. Because it values efficiency over introspection, it has little patience with people's pain. Yet there may be something immensely valuable about the paralysis that marks the passing of passion.

The failures of love usher us into areas of human life that we might never access otherwise—or only access with difficulty. The pain of a breakup pushes the details of our everyday life into the background so that we have no choice but to face our inner demons. We're asked to visit the shadowy cellar that houses our unconscious compulsions. And we're urged to consider what we most value in life and how we might go about attaining it. If we normally rush from task to task without pausing to think, a love failure compels us to slow down and to reflect on how we want to proceed. And because we are likely to feel that we have made a mistake of some kind, we are likely to look carefully and self-critically. We are likely to take a step back and reassess the overall design of our lives. If this design needs readjusting, there's nothing like a broken heart to push us to readjust it. There's nothing like the agony of loss to make us want to actively participate in the shaping of our future.

3

This way of looking at romantic failures revolutionizes how we think about love. As long as we believe that the goal of love is to make us happy, we see romantic ruptures and disappointments as mistakes; we see love's missteps as deviations from its "proper" course. In contrast, when we admit that love's mission might be to mold our destiny, we are able to view its misfortunes as an important part of the process.

Few of us would deny that suffering adds substance to our being. Difficult life experiences refine us, washing away impurities that obscure the core of what we are made of. By this I don't mean that there's an essential kernel of personality hidden within us. But, as I've stressed all along, each of us does have a unique spirit—a distinctive aura or mix of attributes that makes us who we are. This spirit can be weighted down by all manner of superficial preoccupations. Suffering cuts through these layers of redundancy. It strikes at the very heart of being, releasing our spirit from its cage. In this sense, moments when things don't work out well for us are rife with opportunity; they are openings to transformative energies that, in the long run, revitalize our lives.

Let's say you're an optimistic person who isn't too bothered by life's little annoyances and aggravations. You're able to shrug off disappointments better than most of your friends. You don't often dwell in despair. When your friends talk about their troubles, you express sympathy, but you also feel a little disconnected. You don't understand what the big deal is. Likewise, you find it difficult to relate to your boyfriend's bouts of depression. You hate it when he gets all gloomy and self-reflective.

Then your relationship falls apart. Maybe this happens in part exactly because you're not able to meet your partner's pain. Now *you* are in pain. A lot of pain. You don't know how to handle it. It devours your entire world. Every direction you turn, you bump into it. You're a little ashamed so you withdraw from the world. You refuse to see your friends. You don't take calls from your family. You sit with your sadness. You raid your stash of last year's Valentine Day's candy. And you cry and cry and cry. And then you cry some more. You sleep fourteen hours a night. And when you're not sleeping, you're staring at the ceiling, replaying every detail of your failed relationship. Pathetic, right?

Actually, no. Your soul is slowly working its way out of the dank dungeon that it has fallen into. This may take a few weeks or months. Sometimes, if your relationship was truly meaningful, it takes years. When you finally start to come out of it, you may not even realize it at first. If the pain of a breakup is often sudden, hitting you in the gut like a stray bullet, the pace of recovery tends to be sluggish. Unless Robert Pattinson falls down from the sky and drops on one knee, it's going to take some time. But all things in life—good or bad—eventually come to an end. Maybe you wake up one morning and realize that you haven't thought about your ex in a couple of days. Maybe you startle yourself by feeling a tinge of desire for someone else. Maybe the guy who joined your work team two months ago is actually kind of cute. You would have never believed it, but your life does eventually pick up some speed.

It's likely that when you rejoin the land of the living, you won't be living in quite the same way as you were before. When your soul rebuilds itself after having been blown to pieces, the pieces won't always fit back together perfectly.

And you'll need some sort of a strong adhesive to hold them together. This adhesive is often made out of thoughtfulness and compassion. When your friends come to you with their troubles, you know how they feel. Or at least you have a good inkling. Even if you don't always have great advice, you'll have genuine empathy. And when you eventually find a new lover, you won't get anxious when he hits a low frequency. You'll let him rest in the tangle of his despair. Or you'll invite him to share this tangle. You now know how to meet it. Or at least you aren't quite so afraid of not being able to. The fact that you have lost your innocence makes you a better friend and lover. The fact that your own soul is a little battered allows you to deal with the misshapen and suffering souls of others.

4

Does this seem like a consolation prize? It shouldn't. What could be more important than being a good friend and lover? What could be more precious than having a rich and multi-dimensional soul? Not only does such a soul make you feel better about yourself. Not only does it give you confidence that you'll be able to handle more or less any challenge that comes your way. It makes it possible for you to attain higher levels of intimacy with lovers who enter your life after your ordeal. In a way, the pain of past loves makes deeper loves possible in the present. In this instance, the ghosts of the past do not hold you down or derail your plans, as they do when you are caught up in the repetition compulsion. Rather, they animate the space between you and your lover in ways that lend a unique weightiness to your love.

This is one reason I have little patience with the idea that, as women, we should only seek out men who carry no baggage. I honestly think that men who have been wounded in the past make better lovers in the present. Men who have known pain are more interesting, more intense, and more intricate. They may be more complicated—slightly trickier to deal with. But chances are they are also more caring. I tend to be drawn to men with a tad of vulnerability because I know that this vulnerability allows them to access levels of emotional and sexual intimacy that more straightforward men often can't. A lot depends on the state of their pain, of course. If the pain of the past is encased within them unprocessed, without an easy outlet, things may get thorny. Bottled-up pain can give rise to emotional earthquakes that destabilize the foundations of our love. But if this pain has been distilled into thoughtfulness and compassion, it can only augment our relationship; it can only add fibers of fascination to its overall character.

The same goes for your pain. If a mature relationship is what you want, your pain may be your most gifted teacher. If you give it time and space to grow into wisdom, it will open up avenues of relational capacity that would otherwise remain closed to you.

We've learned that there is no way to love without exposing ourselves to the possibility of pain; there is no way to turn passion into something safe and controlled. But this is not a calamity. It's not a tragic flaw in the grand design of love. Quite the contrary, I think it would be an enormous tragedy if we *were* able to safety-proof our love lives. Doing so might spare us some grief, but it would also deprive us of important occasions for actualizing our deepest human potential. It would make it too easy for us to stay shallow and inattentive. It would cheat us of the chance to become the kinds of people others are proud to call their friends and lovers.

Love failures are not life failures. When it comes to love gone wrong, we need to give ourselves a break. We need to give ourselves the permission to fail and to do so spectacularly. We are trained to think that only love that lasts is worthy. I strongly disagree. I think that some of our most far-reaching love affairs are those that fail. With the possible exception of abusive relationships, every love gives us something. And sometimes it's the broken affairs that give us the most. Sometimes our biggest breakdowns lead to our biggest breakthroughs.

This may not be the case immediately. It may be hard to see the upside of things right away. But, over time, the losses of love can give rise to forms of psychological acumen that deepen our character. They can force us to grow layers of strength that we never realized we were capable of. In this sense, there are few mistakes in love. There are no mishaps, but merely fresh opportunities for self-development. In the context of the overall pattern of our lives, it truly is—as the saying goes—better to have loved and lost than never to have loved at all.

In the aftermath of a failed love affair, it's easy to admonish ourselves for having been so imprudent. It's easy to see only a shameful blunder. We should have known better than to trust that man! We should have taken greater care with our heart! We should not have invested ourselves so thoroughly! But such statements often (not always, but often) represent an overly cursory assessment of what love is supposed to accomplish. And they also overlook something absolutely fundamental about love, namely that it's often inherently transient. Sometimes men behave like jerks—no doubt about it. But most of our love affairs don't end because men make appalling lovers. They end, quite simply, because most loves are not meant to last (more on this in Chapter 12). Once they deliver their message, they move on, leaving us to decode that message as best we can. Telling ourselves that the broken affair was a mistake from beginning to end will not in any way help us crack the mysterious code of passion.

We tend to think that it's the weak who get scorched by love—that the strong know how to protect themselves. But I suspect that frequently the reverse is the case. I suspect that it's often the strong who get positively pummeled by love. This is because they are the ones willing to take the risk of getting hurt in the first place. The weak recoil from robust love because they realize that the more intensely they love, the more likely they are to get singed. They keep love at a safe distance because they're not sure they would survive a truly devastating heartbreak. Sometimes they walk away from a relationship the moment it gets in any way fiery or consequential. This is often called commitment-phobia. I call it cowardice.

Love is not made for the faint-hearted. It's not made for those who hesitate on the sidelines. You must be tremendously brave, tremendously audacious, to throw yourself into the eye of the hurricane. You must have incredible faith in your ability to mend a broken heart to risk falling into the arms of a lover whose motivations you might never fully understand. In a deep sense, passion is meant for the resilient—for those who know that they'll find their way back onto solid ground no matter how badly they fall. It's meant for those who are confident that love's disappointments won't ravage them beyond repair. And it's meant for those who recognize that sometimes a massive love followed by a massive failure is more glorious than a timidly lived success.

We're often told that those who have been traumatized in the past—and particularly those with difficult childhoods— end up taking imprudent romantic risks because they have never learned to love properly. Their wounds, supposedly, lead them to hurtful lovers. Their injuries cause them to court demeaning affairs. This may sometimes be the case. We've seen that the repetition compulsion has an eerie ability to land us in one painful relationship after another. There are definitely times when the ravenous ghosts of our past guide us to people who are not good for us. But it may also be that those who have endured a lot of pain are willing to take romantic risks because they are, ultimately, less afraid than those who haven't.

5

I am asking you to reevaluate the meaning of past pain.

I would be the last person to deny that the past impacts the present. I know that a traumatizing past can make it tough to avoid trauma in the present. Those who are grappling with difficult personal histories may need to work harder at love than those with golden childhoods. They may have specific vulnerabilities to overcome—specific fault lines to protect. There may be particular relationship scenarios that cause them to unravel. However, I'm convinced that, in a more general sense, those who have experienced pain tend to be more resourceful than those who haven't. Those who have survived hopelessness know how to hope. When they fall into despair, they know that there will be light at the end of the tunnel. They know this because they have been in that tunnel before. They have found their way out before, so they have faith that they can do it again. They have a realistic sense of what it takes to overcome pain. And thus they overcome it more consistently than those who have had less practice.

I don't mean to glorify trauma. It's just that I think that it's useful to question our habitual understanding of pain. In our therapeutic culture, it's common to see pain as something that damages a person for life. An individual who has gone through traumatic experiences is supposed to be somehow "maimed," unable to enter into the swing of things with the same ease as those who have been more fortunate. In the same way that an alcoholic is always an alcoholic, an emotionally damaged person, allegedly, never fully transcends his or her damage. There's a sense in which this is true. Damage is not something that you can ever fully brush aside. It will always be a part of your psychological makeup. But there are ways to live with past damage that make you a more full-bodied person. There are ways to knit pain into the tapestry of your life so that this tapestry becomes more durable, more able to withstand adversity. On this view, pain doesn't necessarily generate more pain. Rather, it makes you tougher, and therefore more willing to accept a gamble. It gives you the certainty that no matter how imperfectly things will turn out, you'll have the emotional suppleness to bounce back.

The "once a victim, always a victim" mentality of our culture can blind us to this. It can keep wounded people from recognizing their strength. And it can cause those around them to patronize them. There's little that's more annoying than the condescension of those who haven't experienced half of your hardship but who take it upon themselves to "instruct" you on the right ways to handle suffering. Such people often assume that they are stronger than you are because they haven't been broken by pain. And they assume that this "strength" gives them the right to judge your way of coping with relationship dramas. Until they themselves slip and fall. Then they'll run to you for comfort because they know that you'll understand what they're going through. And you do. But you also realize what they might not, namely that there's no easy fix. There's no expedient way to cast off pain. The only way out is straight through it.

Those who are intimately familiar with pain know that suppressing it will only make things worse. They understand that they must let pain take up its rightful place among other emotions. Doing so doesn't make them weak. Instead, it's a sign that they have enough inner spaciousness to allow pain to coexist with their more cheerful sentiments.

People who don't know how to welcome pain in this way either pretend that it's not there or try to force it out by all manner of trivial distractions. They refuse to listen to its messages. As a result, they miss out on its lessons. Worse still, because they can't allow themselves to feel their pain, they often also can't tolerate yours. They'll show contempt for your attempts to greet pain with the respect it deserves. They don't realize that it's a thousand times more difficult to look pain straight in the face than to smother it under false displays of strength. They don't fully grasp that a person who is capable of feeling great pain is also capable of feeling great joy. In the same way that the ordinary doesn't cancel out the extraordinary, pain doesn't cancel out joy. It's merely one of joy's many preconditions.

You can feel pain without being ruled by it. You can accept it without being shattered by it. You can honor it without being indebted to it. Those with genuine emotional intelligence understand this. They're not afraid of the more somber shades of life. And they know that our culture is mistaken in trying to sanitize love by turning it into something as wholesome as a Kellogg's oatmeal bar. You're supposed to reach for this bar whenever you get a craving for chocolate. The problem is that when you're salivating over a luscious slice of chocolate cake, no oatmeal bar in the world is going to satisfy you. Likewise with passion.

Passion is not meant to allow you to lead a healthy and balanced life. It's meant to throw you off-kilter and make you a little fanatical. It doesn't have much respect for folks who tiptoe to the edge of a deep connection only to pull back at the last moment. It doesn't have a high opinion of those who settle for second-rate marriages in order to guarantee their security. Real passion admits that love is a matter of playing with humongous stakes. It knows that the opposite of great love is not indifference. It's great pain.

Love doesn't aim at unhappiness. But it doesn't necessarily aim at happiness either. Failure is not the antithesis of love. It's merely the other side of the coin. When you flip a coin, you can never predict whether it's heads or tails you'll end up with. What's worse, someone has flooded the market with fake coins that have no heads. So your odds aren't even 50/50. If you chance upon one of these fake coins, you can't win. The coin will always land on tails. But there's no way to know this ahead of time. The forgeries are so clever that they pass for the real thing until the last moment, when the coin is already in the air. As a result, the only way to tell the difference between a fake coin and a real one is to toss it. While both can land on tails—while both can spell defeat—the real ones enrich your life even when they do.

If your coin lands on tails but you're able to pick up the thread of your life as if nothing had happened, it's likely that the coin was fake. It didn't have much purchasing power. But if you're forced to reconsider the framework of your existence, you may have held in your hand an authentic gold coin. Our loves can be more or less successful, but the ones that are genuinely transformative are never counterfeit. Such loves glow with a radiance that persists long after we have lost them.

CHAPTER 11

....

Mourning Well Is Living Well

> **MYTH:** Mourning a love loss weakens us.
>
> **FACT:** In the long run, mourning strengthens us by giving us access to fresh forms of life.

1

We live in a culture that is filled with stuff. And we learn early that much of this stuff is easily replaceable. If I don't like the toothpaste I picked up at the store, I can go back the next day and buy something better. If I want to, I can spend an hour in the toothpaste aisle meditating on the respective strengths of Colgate versus Aquafresh.

One of the biggest problems with our current romantic culture is that it encourages us to treat our relationships in much the same way. Do you suspect that the man you're with might be somehow defective? That he might have some unresolved issues? Well, don't waste your time. Get rid of him and find yourself a better one! You deserve the best. You deserve someone who is able to express his feelings clearly and emphatically. No mixed signals, please. Even if you yourself suffer from all kinds of relationship doubts, your guy should be free of all such obstacles. And he should know at all times that he's easily replaceable.

The trouble is, people are not easily replaceable. There are aspects of the Internet era that lead us to believe that they are. Dating sites such as match.com give us the impression that there is a romantic equivalent to the toothpaste aisle. We can spend days shopping for the right man on such sites. Browsing photos and personal profiles is not that different from the process of figuring out which toothpaste will most brighten our smile.

I'm not saying that there's something inherently wrong with dating sites. I know a few people who have been able to find wonderful partners through them. Yet they do contribute to a romantic culture that increasingly treats love as yet another commodity. You choose your partner based on a standardized set of attributes that he's able to offer. You can go on as many first dates as you want before committing to anything, in just the same way as you can test-drive as many cars as you want before making your final selection. And the similarities between dating sites and car dealerships don't end here. Both have a way of making the newest model look more attractive than what you already have. They tempt you to trade in your old model as soon as it starts to show signs of wear.

I have myself told you that you should get out of relationships that are abusive or demeaning—that a bad romance can only diminish you. But this is different from the car-dealership mentality I'm talking about. This mentality, unfortunately, doesn't prepare us for the fact that some of the people we love are absolutely irreplaceable. Anyone who has experienced a genuine loss knows this. Sure, we can usually, over time, find someone else to love. We may eventually find someone even more compelling. The failures of love, as I've argued, are often openings to something more satisfying. Many of us ultimately come to the conclusion that we're better off without the lover we have lost. But this doesn't change the fact that some of our losses are irredeemable. There are lovers who touch us on such a profound level that their value is incalculable. When we lose one of them, we can't log onto match.com to find another copy. He is matchless—beyond replication.

Few things in life are more agonizing than giving up a person who feels irreplaceable to us. It's good to admit this. It's good to acknowledge that mourning a lost love is demanding. Sometimes our life is so snugly intertwined with that of our lover that it's impossible to detangle ourselves without major wounding. We'll bleed for a long time. And the scarring will be considerable. There may even be times when our mourning never fully ends—when the recollection of a lost lover lingers on indefinitely. We may do our best to repress it. We may refuse to think about him. We may bury ourselves in our work. We may move to a different city, or even a different country. We may honestly feel that we have been able to get on with our lives. But then, one day, we catch a familiar note of music. Or we remember how Vermont smells after a summer storm. The memories come flooding back. Even when we have poured all of our strength into fleeing the past, it has a way of catching up with us whenever our defenses are down.

2

Those we have loved ardently leave behind a lasting legacy. Our inner world will forever hold their trace. We will forever feel their presence. And the course of our future is in some ways influenced by that presence. Even though our lost lover is no longer a part of our everyday reality, he has a role to play in the overall direction of our lives. In this sense, loss does not always signal an end to a relationship. It can be the beginning of a different kind of alliance—one that recognizes the enduring significance of those we have lost.

This kind of an alliance with a lost lover can feel as substantial as the bonds we form with new lovers. Granted, we may not always feel its presence very strongly. We may get so caught up in the urgencies of our new life that it falls into the background. Yet we are aware that somewhere in the folds of our being it persists. The nostalgic imprint of a life that we might have had survives even as our new life engages our attention. And during those moments when our new life fails to fully absorb us, we revisit the life that we have left behind. During moments such as these, we get lost in the reverie of what could, should, or might have been. We feel that melancholy pang of regret that we had hoped to overcome a long time ago.

Mourning respects this pang. It knows that the legacy of

powerful passions can make a real contribution to our lives. This is why it actively encourages us to carry a vestige of our lost loves into our future. Here's a concrete example: I once dated a wonderful man who was an efficient writer. He was much younger than I was. But while I sat at my desk suffering from a writer's block, he routinely churned out twenty pages in one sitting. I was amused. But I was also a little annoyed at myself. What was the use of all my experience if I couldn't get any of my ideas onto the written page? Nothing much changed while I dated this man. But after the breakup—which was an immense loss to me—I noticed something. When I sat down to write, I actually wrote. Not twenty pages a day. But a good five pages. That was more than ten years ago and I haven't stopped writing since. I don't know how it happened. But I do know that somehow I inherited this man's level-headed attitude toward writing. I've always wanted to thank him for this gift, which, all things considered, is enormous. I lost the man but kept one of the qualities that most appealed to me.

In most cases, the qualities we "steal" from a lover after a breakup are not quite as tangible as this. More often, they are emotional tonalities that somehow, in the process of mourning, become a part of our psychological constitution. Even though such tonalities connect us to our past, they also help us renew ourselves for the purposes of our future. They expand the boundaries of our private world. They add fresh attributes to our mental repertoire. Because we cannot insert new characters into our inner drama without revamping the whole play, they make us more versatile, more multifaceted. From this perspective, our personality is a storehouse of characteristics that we have accumulated through our losses. It reflects the history of these losses as much as the network of our current relationships. Who we are at any given point of our lives is in part determined by the kinds of people we have been forced to give up. In a way, the more we have lost, the more substantial our identities. One might even say that a psyche that has not experienced loss is not a fully realized psyche.

If this is the case, isn't there also the possibility that we internalize the negative characteristics of those we have lost? I'm afraid so. There's always the danger of becoming heir to the worst features of those we have loved. This is one reason it's important to be discriminating about the sorts of people we let into our lives in the first place.

That said, there is perhaps a lesser chance of soaking up negative qualities than positive ones because we are usually consciously trying to fend them off. Let's say your ex is judgmental. And let's say this is why the two of you broke up. In the wake of the breakup, you're likely to revisit moments when your ex was disapproving. But you're unlikely to internalize this trait because you find it annoying. You may in fact be so angry about it that you deliberately go in the opposite direction. You work on becoming as indulgent as you possibly can. This may backfire in various ways. And that unwanted tendency to be hypercritical may sneak in anyway through the back door of your unconscious. But it's likely that your resistance to it is quite high.

When it comes to "negative" qualities, it's much more probable that you'll inherit a weakness than something that makes you angry. This "weakness" could be a trauma of some sort or a depressive tendency. But my sense is that this would be a real danger only if your alliance was very long-lasting, such as a twenty-year marriage. In that case, your relationship to your ex would be akin to your relationship to your family of origin. You might be susceptible to what theoreticians describe as "intergenerational transmission of trauma." This refers to the fact that we can embrace the traumas of our parents, and even of our grandparents, without knowing it. Because of our proximity to our parents for so many years, it's easy to adopt their blueprints of suffering. It's easy to begin to carry their depression or their addiction—which they, in turn, may have taken over from their own parents.

My friend Julie has an interesting example: The highly distinctive pattern of her chronic back pain is identical to the pattern of her mother's back pain. Julie knows that her pain is largely psychosomatic. As a consequence, if her pain is inherited (as she believes), it's likely that whatever psychological issues are motivating it are also motivating her mother's pain.

3

The reason our loved ones can have such a huge impact on us is that our psyches are inherently porous. We are open to the world in ways that make it impossible to distinguish between the inside and the outside, the psychic and the social. This openness ensures our aliveness; it allows the revitalizing energies of the world to infiltrate our being so that we remain psychologically agile. But it also makes us susceptible to hazardous influences.

Some of these influences are impersonal. The noise and commotion of big cities can get under our skin. The freezing temperatures of the winter can make our bodies tense up. Our neighbor's blaring radio can drive us to distraction. What unites such experiences is that we have little control over them. And they tend to make us feel overstimulated, as if we were fending off a hostile attack. Those who are lucky enough to have the financial resources to do so often seek a refuge or an antidote of some sort. They flee to the peace of the countryside, they take a trip to the Bahamas, or they find a soundproof condo. The rest of us manage as best we can. We learn to cope with such assaults. But they do, over time, take a toll.

Think of how much more this is the case when we are dealing with deeply personal connections with people we adore. It's a cliché that people we most love often hurt us the most. Insofar as love equals openness, there's no way around this. Among the many ironies of life is that the more open (and thus alive) we are, the more intensely vulnerable we become.

It's not surprising, therefore, that one of the first things that happens when a relationship ends painfully is that we clam up. We retreat to our castle, pull up the drawbridge, position soldiers at the ramparts, and slam the iron door shut. This is necessary; it's smart to seek cover when we are wounded. Our rush to place limits on our openness blocks the influx of harmful outside influences—particularly those originating from our ex. It allows us to shift our focus from him back to ourselves. As we all know, breakups make us self-absorbed. No matter how self-deprecating we get, our sadness causes us to center on ourselves. Sometimes we dwell on our dejection in ways that might, at first glance, seem largely counterproductive. But, actually, being a little selfish is an essential part of mourning.

Here is why. When we love, the bulk of our energies is aimed at our lover. Freud had a fancy word for this: cathexis. Cathexis is a form of bonding. We can be cathected to pretty much anything: Our jobs, some creative activity, the television screen, meditation, exercise, friends, our dog, or neighborhood gossip. Even alcohol or drug addiction is a form of cathexis. But there's nothing that cathects our energies as effectively as love. Through romantic love, we bond intensely with another person. Energies that are usually available for other ends—such as our job or exercise—are directed at our lover. This is why we tend to put our hobbies and fitness routines on the back burner when we fall in love. The end of love is agonizing in part because it asks us to "decathect" our energies. It asks us to withdraw our investment in our lover and to cathect to other details of our lives instead. Because mourning focuses our attention back on the self, it helps us accomplish this.

Sometimes sadness itself turns into a cathexis. This is

when depression becomes unremitting and long-term. On the surface, this may seem senseless. Why would we want to bond to our sadness? But when our lives seem completely empty, when there appears to be nothing worth living for, sadness may be the only thing we can hold onto. It's something concrete—something that fills our days. As a result, it can become a counterintuitive (yet powerful) way to give structure to our existence.

When things get this far, there's nothing as scary as letting go of our sadness. This is because on the far side of it is a total void. Even misery is better than this void. Earlier in this book, I talked about a foundational lack at the heart of human life. That lack is inescapable. The emotional void we experience after a love failure is related to it in the sense that what we have lost is a person who promised to return our Thing to us; we have lost a person who promised us wholeness. But the post-breakup void is also more drastic, more insistent, than our everyday malaise. It's harder to cover up with distractions. It's so gaping that we find it difficult to convince ourselves that we could ever fill it. So, sometimes, we stop trying to. We surrender ourselves to our sadness.

What's tricky about this is that it's often impossible to tell the difference between sadness that is working toward an outlet and sadness that has become an end in itself. When we're in the midst of our despair, it's hard to know whether we are undergoing a necessary phase of mourning, or whether we have become so enmeshed in our depression that we're hurting ourselves. While the former will augment us, the latter might in the long run impoverish us. It might imprison us in a solipsistic bubble that impedes further evolution by shutting out the external world. This is something to keep in mind when weighing the pros and cons of antidepressants. If we take drugs to mask the symptoms of normal mourning, we frustrate the process of personal development that such mourning is meant to carry out. But if we take drugs to break a cycle of interminable depression, we may jump-start that process by opening a much-needed space for outside influences.

The problem with overly long periods of sadness is that they cause us to build impenetrable barriers around ourselves. Our solitary castle becomes a permanent abode. Not only do we cut off all avenues of approach; we erect extra barricades and hire a whole battalion of new soldiers to fend off any outside threat. Over time, we assemble a shield—what Freud described as a deadened "crust"—that keeps the inner layers of our self protected against external stimuli. In a way, we sacrifice the aliveness of our outer self in order to protect the viability of our inner self. We become so tightly guarded that we start to harden; we lose our elasticity and capacity for transformation. It's true that the more we numb ourselves against the world, the fewer of its destructive influences get through. But the penalty we pay for this is that we begin to atrophy from a lack of restorative energies. Our private world remains sheltered. But our personality slowly freezes over. Indeed, when you meet a person whose way of being in the world seems unusually cold or robotic, there's a good chance that he or she is protecting a vulnerable core.

4

To avoid this predicament, we must allow ourselves to feel our pain. And we must admit that lovers don't only change us when they enter our lives; they also change us when they leave. When we mourn a lost relationship, we not only mourn the lover who has died, left, or betrayed us. We mourn the version of ourselves that he helped bring into being. Although we craft ourselves in relation to our friends, family, careers, goals, ambitions, and other important aspects of our lives, lovers are a particularly charged piece of our practice of self-fashioning. The self we construct through an intimate connection to a loved one is significantly different from the self we would have without him. Consequently, when we lose this lover, we are not only tempted to adopt some of his characteristics. We are also forced to undo some of the inner structures that his presence generated (and that may have come to feel comfortable to us); we are asked to discard outdated parts of our being. We cannot, in short, give up a lover without entering into a lengthy process of psychological reconfiguration.

A romantic failure urges us to reconceive who we are. We may curse ourselves for not being able to do so quickly enough. And we may feel embarrassed about how unbearable our loss feels. But sometimes there are good reasons for our reluctance to overcome our loss. It's possible that we're struggling so much because our lost lover has directed us onto a life-path that's actually right for us—that we *should* be on. It's conceivable that he has helped us become a better version of ourselves. In such instances, our sadness is not merely a means of honoring our lost love. It connects us to potentialities of our being that we need to safeguard. I'm talking about those potentialities that were energized by our love and that are therefore threatened by its loss. A big part of mourning is finding ways to nourish these potentialities outside the broken relationship. It's only when we learn to thrive beyond the confines of that relationship that it's safe for us to finally let go of it.

Mourning is a paradoxical process. On the one hand, it causes us to fixate on what we have lost. On the other, it aims to allow us to go on with our lives without the lover who once meant so much to us; it aims to enable us to gradually release our grip on our ex so that we can, in time, love again. When we first start to mourn, we usually can't tolerate the idea of replacing our lost love with a new one. The intensity of our suffering prevents this. Our pain forges a powerful bond to our ex. It delays the final rupture. It functions as a display of faithfulness that signals that we have not severed the emotional ties that attach us to the lover we're mourning. In this fashion, pain seeks to stretch love past its expiration date—to keep our ex from sliding into oblivion. Intuitively we know that when we transcend our pain, we also transcend our relationship. No wonder, then, that we often find it difficult to finish the process of mourning. We would rather feel pain than face the irrevocable loss that its absence signifies.

It's easy to feel that the better we bear the failure of our relationship, the more we betray the person we have lost. Yet mourning demands that we, eventually, give ourselves the permission to start feeling better. If we cannot do this—if we cannot find a way out of our pain—we also cannot find our way to new passions. We cannot begin to redirect our desire toward new objects. The moment our desire leaps toward something unknown is the fork in the road that allows us to veer away from our lost love. Even if we can still steal glimpses of this love from our new path, we are now ready to welcome new lovers into our lives. As I've emphasized, these new lovers might never fully replace the lost one. But they will over time begin to take up more and more of our attention. They will gradually blunt the memory of what we have lost.

5

Mourning is not just designed to make life possible after loss. It's designed to make *new* forms of life available to us. This, in turn, means that if we don't know how to mourn, we don't know how to live. If we don't know how to shed old skin, we don't know how to bring new editions of ourselves into being.

I've suggested that love's failures arrest us in our steps, forcing us to take a close look at our lives. This is an important part of the process. But, unless we're willing to let our pain solidify into interminable depression, we must ultimately find the strength to start moving again. We must find the strength to catch the cadence of life from an unfamiliar spot. We must insert ourselves into it from a new place and in a new way.

The strenuous itinerary of mourning is meant to guarantee that we, in due course, manage to do so. It forces us to take our time because it knows that moving too quickly from one phase of our lives to the next will undermine the process. This is why it takes patience. Its gifts are slow to flower. We cannot conjure up new forms of life out of a void. We need first to assemble new supplies and fresh sources of strength.

There are times when we try to short-circuit this process—when we try to get around pain by pretending that our loss is not a big deal. We may even fill our lives with meaningless love affairs to prove this to ourselves. But when we take such a shortcut, we make it impossible for ourselves to complete the journey. We end up trying to move forward with outdated tools; we approach the present moment with resources that were intended for an earlier stage of our lives. In contrast, when we allow ourselves to mourn, we progressively accumulate the tools and resources that we need for a life that is drastically unlike the one we're used to.

In a way, it's only when our present reality becomes so rich (so full of new tools and resources) that it manages to fully engross our attention that we can stop obsessing about the past. New passions—new ambitions and preoccupations—have a way of forcing out old ones. Even injuries are easy to forget and forgive when our lives are teeming with new opportunities. In this sense, it's not that we need to overcome the past in order to bring about a future. It's that we are able to transcend the past when we become so committed to something in the future that our commitment eclipses the pain of the past.

Mourning well is living well. When we know how to mourn, we understand that loss is rarely a pure loss. As I indicated in the previous chapter, there is usually something we get in return for our romantic investments. There's normally a compensation for the pain we are asked to endure. This compensation finds its way into our lives during the time it takes us to travel from the spot where loss punches us in the stomach to the spot where we start breathing again. This distance is exhausting to traverse. But it's also much more packed with insight than most other periods of our existence. Make no mistake. This insight is part of our compensation. It hastens our evolution. It makes up for those stretches of life when we languish in a limbo—when not a whole lot happens.

Because we don't progress at an even or smooth pace, life events that jolt us to a higher level of maturity are invaluable. Heartbreak is among these. It's one of those watershed moments that accelerate our overall development. This is why those who have hit rock-bottom are usually more fascinating than those who haven't. Think of it this way: Older people are wise not only because they have lived longer. They're wise because they have lost more. They have had more watershed moments, more forks in the road.

How we cope with the aftermath of loss has a huge impact on our destiny. We can either stay stuck in our sadness. Or we can steadily burrow our way out of it. It is a tribute to the nimbleness of the human spirit that we usually find ways to translate loss into meaning. As a matter of fact, we sometimes discover that what most devastated us in the past becomes the cornerstone of our future. This is because we never quite know what the future holds. We understand that each of our actions in the present initiates a slightly different future. Yet the outline of our lives is so meandering that there's no way to immediately assess the long-term ramifications of any of our actions; we never know in advance how our current choices will impact what's to come.

Sometimes it takes years for us to fully grasp the significance of a particular event or life trial. The decision we thought would benefit us lands us in a muddle? But the one we always regretted making ends up bringing a reward? The only thing that's certain is that each cast of the die has repercussions that we can't anticipate. There may be ways to calculate some probabilities. There may even be some strategies that increase our chances for a good future. But, ultimately, we never know what's waiting around the bend.

Are you having trouble getting over a lover you lost three years ago? Do you fear that you'll never meet anyone else who can even begin to compare? I know how that feels. But who is to say that someone even more marvelous isn't fated to cross your path? When you're in the throes of grief, it's hard to believe this. But the great thing about human beings is that one amazing specimen doesn't cancel out others equally amazing. Each one is remarkable in his or her special way. Each one emits a luster that's slightly different from all others.

The fact that a given lover is irreplaceable doesn't mean that you can't find others who are just as exquisite. No matter how specific your desire is—and we've seen that it can be very specific—you're bound to meet more than one man who resonates on the right frequency. And you may find that the loss you thought was intolerable is what makes it possible for one of these men to enter your life. You may find that your disappointment was merely a prelude to something magical that you're only able to attain through that disappointment. I'm not saying that you're powerless in the face of fate—that you can't influence how your life turns out. But there's such a thing as knowing when something is beyond your control. And there's such a thing as recognizing that loss often holds the seeds of a new beginning. Life has a way of turning things around. Those who mourn well know this. As a result, they also live well—with courage and curiosity.

CHAPTER 12

....

What Is Meant to Happen
Always Will

> **MYTH:** We can prolong our relationships
> by making a greater effort.
>
> **FACT:** Sometimes it's better to lose a love than to
> stifle it with anxious attempts to keep it alive.

1

If there's one thing I would like you to take away from this book, it's the idea that we cannot control the course of romance. In making my case for falling in love, I have emphasized that because love is so complicated, our approach to it needs to be simple. The best we can do is to step right into it, surrender to it, experience it, and learn from it regardless of how it turns out. There are always complex reasons for why our loves either thrive or fail. It's unlikely that we'll ever entirely grasp these reasons. If anything, the more doggedly we strive to, the more exhausted we get. We end up dissipating our energies on trying to make sense of emotional opacities that resist clarity. In contrast, when we embrace the mysteries of love without worrying too much about where we will wind up, we create space for uncontrived intimacy. We open ourselves to authentic romantic encounters that enrich our lives a lot more than schemes of relationship manipulation ever could. Love, after all, is not a formula. It's messy. And in its messiness resides its power to captivate us.

The more vigilant we become about romance, the less dynamically we're able to love. By this I don't mean that we shouldn't work on cultivating good relationships, or that there isn't anything we can do to foster intimacy. We do have a lot of control over how we treat our lovers and how we negotiate the details of closeness. And we can set clear boundaries on what is acceptable to us within a relationship. It's just that when it comes to the final destiny of our passions, there isn't much we can do. We can't force a man to love us. We can't force him to make a commitment. We can't even force him to stay the night. We can't artificially extend the shelf life of our love. Deep-freezing it won't work. Nor will reheating it. When it's done, it's done. All of our efforts to prevent the inevitable can only frustrate us. In the realm of romance, it's best to accept that what is meant to happen always will—that there isn't much to be gained from struggling against the undertow of our romantic destinies.

Our self-help culture tries to persuade us otherwise. It tries to tell us that there are strategies we can implement that will ensure the longevity of our relationships. Nothing could be less productive. We cannot stage-manage our love lives so that we always come out on top. Human relationships possess the kind of density that evades our grip. Although we can learn to better navigate this density, we'll never master it. And the more arrogant we become—the more we convince ourselves that we can trick love into yielding its secrets—the more likely we are to fall flat on our face. As a result, if there's a piece of concrete advice in this book, it's that you will benefit if you nurture your capacity to tolerate love's murky stretches.

There's not much that makes you more powerful in love than your ability to meet its ambiguities, uncertainties, confusions, and surprises with a degree of resourcefulness. This is where the battle should be waged: Not between you and your lover, but within your own being. There's no better protection than knowing that your heart is strong enough (and your life is full enough) to survive the utter untidiness of love.

2

I've stressed that to love is to accept the possibility of failure. This may be hard to hear. It may be tempting to reach for that self-help book that outlines the twelve steps guaranteed to solve your relationship problems. But consider the freedom that comes from giving up the effort to force your love into a predesignated pattern. Again, I'm not advocating passivity. I'm not saying that you should sit back with folded arms while your relationship unravels. As I argued in Chapter 9, every relationship has its difficulties. Every love affair awakens the hungry ghosts of the past. And every one of us needs to cope with the recurring patterns of the repetition compulsion. But there's a difference between trying to work through a specific issue on the one hand and trying to secure your lover's affections on the other. Either he loves you or he doesn't. End of story. There's no ruse you can implement to inflame his flagging fervor. There's no ploy you can devise to ensure the finale that you might want (such as marriage). If anything, the more you plot, the less you're able to relax into your relationship. The more you worry about the future of your love, the less you're able to embrace its here and now.

Think of it this way. Will you enjoy sex more if you let yourself get caught up in the momentum of your passion? Or when you climb into bed with a guide that outlines the twelve biggest sex mistakes women make? In all likelihood, your guide will paralyze you to the point of defeating the whole idea of having sex. You might as well curl up with a good book and a cup of hot chocolate instead. The same goes for relationships. The idea of applying twelve steps to your relationship is no more ridiculous than that of applying them to sex. But it's easier to see the ridiculousness when it comes to sex. We know that the more utilitarian our approach to sex, the less likely we are to enjoy it. Yet love is no more designed for our systems of control than sex is. Eros is profoundly irrational. It has no interest in the betterment of society. It's not invested in progress. It follows no evolutionary imperative. It's not even interested in your well-being. It challenges any and all attempts to render it predictable. And you know what? This is why we like it—this is why we love to love. Love is so delightful because it's *not* rational.

When we attempt to turn love into something rational,

we diminish its power to inflame us. It's impossible to feel inspired about something we're trying to manipulate. Romantic relationships are living and breathing entities. They need living and breathing responses. Tactics that are imported from the outside, from some book of rules, can only stifle them. And, ultimately, trying to tame love is as deceptive as trying to tame a tiger. You may succeed for a while. You may get lulled into the false security of thinking that your tiger is as harmless as your neighbor's sweet kitty-cat.

This was the mistake Roy Horn, the famous tamer of tigers, made at the Mirage in Las Vegas. He stepped into the tiger's cage thinking he was safe. What did Mr. Tiger do? He mauled the brave tamer to shreds. Love, like Bengal tigers, is fickle. Institutions such as marriage are designed to contain it. But if we're totally honest with ourselves, we know that there's no human institution that can discipline it. Institutions promise security. But they can never guarantee it. Sometimes, when we're least prepared for it, love breaks out of its cage and runs for the hills.

When we try to control love, it's usually because we're trying to keep ourselves from getting hurt. This is understandable. It makes sense that we would do everything in our power to prevent pain. Sadly, we can't. In some ways, our biggest mistake is to expect safety from a force that's by definition unreliable. We might fare better if we took it for granted that love is made of contradictions and sudden reversals. This doesn't mean that all loves are inconsistent. Some of us manage to forge durable and even-keeled relationships.

However, it's just as likely that our alliance fails for no apparent reason. Desire may inexplicably die. Our partner may suddenly withdraw. Or we may ourselves long for freedom. This is sometimes the case even when everything seems fine on the surface. We may feel suffocated even though our lover has in no way restricted our freedom. Or our lover may feel compelled to flee even though he still loves us. In such instances, those who expect permanence from their relationships will suffer tremendously. In contrast, those who are used to the idea of upheaval will find it easier to let go. They may be just as wounded, but they'll be more prepared for the possibility of love ending without warning.

I've proposed that love that lasts is an exception. Loss is the rule. The possibility of loss is woven into the cloth of each of our loves from the very beginning. Indeed, it's because love is inherently precarious that it's so precious to us in the first place. It's because we know that we could lose it at any moment that we value it so much. When you think about it, many of the things we most cherish in life are fleeting. Even delicate wildflowers are treasured in part because they won't last beyond the season. Understanding this makes it easier to endure love's inevitable ruptures. On the one hand, it makes us more appreciative of passion while it lasts. On the other, it ensures that we won't be too surprised when love comes to a full stop.

Letting a lover walk away before we are ready to let him go is one of the hardest things many of us will ever do. Accepting that love is often intrinsically ephemeral might facilitate this task. If nothing else, it might keep us from blaming our-selves for things that are beyond our control. It might help us remember that love can die without us having done anything to kill it.

3

The awareness that we could lose our love at any moment isn't an impediment to being able to love. It's merely its solemn underside. And, as I have sought to show in this book, love can be meaningful even when it doesn't last. Some of our most memorable, most enthralling love affairs are ones that don't endure. We shouldn't feel apologetic about this. It all depends on how you think about the matter. If you expect a lavish wedding, two kids, a house in the suburbs, a white picket fence, a dog and two cats, you'll think yourself a failure if you end up having a series of ardent but short-lived affairs instead. But if you value passion over security, you might decide that the latter is actually a better deal. I don't have any interest in telling you to think one way or other. What you want from love is your own business. But it's useful to recog-nize that there are various ways to measure the "success" of your relationships. Whether or not you think of yourself as successful depends on what you choose to appreciate.

The notion that a romantic relationship should last an entire lifetime may well be a remnant of a different cultural arrangement. It's a vestige of a time when the stability of the family was necessary for the stability of the social order.

Times have changed. There are those who lament the loss of family values, but it's simply not the case that our social order will collapse if people keep getting divorced. And we certainly have enough children to populate the world. There are much more pressing cultural and political problems than the decline of the family. From terrorism to environmental concerns, our society is tackling problems that earlier generations could not have imagined. These problems have little to do with people's love lives. Moreover, fewer people these days stay together merely because they think they're socially expected to. From where I'm looking, this is cause for celebration. It leads to more sincere relationships. I like to know that my partner stays with me because he wants to rather than because he thinks that he's culturally obligated to.

This of course doesn't change the fact that many of us want life-long relationships. There's nothing wrong with that. And if we get lucky, our wish may even be granted. But this shouldn't make us overlook the possibility that there are loves that "succeed" precisely because they end. Permanent relationships can be the greatest thing that ever happened to us. But they can also become insipid over time. Sometimes it's better to lose a love than to watch our passion turn into a faint shadow of its former self.

Wherever we turn in our culture, we're told that sustaining passion over time takes effort—that we should do everything in our power to keep desire alive. But, truthfully, sometimes letting passion run its course is better than putting it on life support. Aren't we already working hard enough? Why do our love lives also have to become a site of endless exertion? Particularly when it's unlikely that our efforts will pay off? One of the paradoxes of love is that our attempts to render it stable tend to suppress the spirit of improvisation that makes it so enjoyable to begin with. Our protective measures can cause us to lose the very thing we're trying to protect; they can destroy the very ardor that initially mesmerized us.

Undoubtedly, it's often difficult to let romance unfold to its natural rhythm. Admitting that our efforts to dictate love's course are usually a misguided attempt to force it to last beyond its intended span may make it easier for us to loosen our hold. It may make it possible for us to allow bewildering relationship scenarios to exhaust themselves on their own.

Take the painful scenario I introduced above: Your lover decides to leave you even though he still loves you. You press him for a reason. He keeps saying that he doesn't have a good one. Well, it may actually be that he doesn't know why he wants out. He may himself be perplexed by his own conflicting feelings. Like you, he's a constantly evolving entity. His inner world reconfigures itself on a regular basis. His feelings wax and wane. By the time he begins to "understand" one version of himself, another one has already come into existence. It's therefore not that surprising that he may one morning wake up not being entirely sure how he feels. Even if he knows that he wants something different, he may not know what that might be. Or why he wants it. The pull toward freedom may be deeply intuitive, without any logical basis. In such cases, it doesn't help to insist on explanations, for they, quite simply, don't exist. If he gave you one, he would be lying.

A lover's unreadability can make us anxious. It adds yet another layer of uncertainty to our relationship. It may even cause us to jump to erroneous conclusions about how he feels because imagining that we know is more reassuring than admitting that we don't. Particularly when we're dealing with a disagreement, it's easy to believe that understanding our partner will help us heal the rift. This is true in the sense that seeing where he is coming from may help us better relate to him. However, when our quest for clarity begins to serve as a way to deny his uncertainty, it becomes impinging. If what he needs to express is ambivalence, our rush to impose an interpretation on him can suppress his authentic feelings; it can get in the way of truthful communication. For instance, when we assume that he is like us—that he is reacting the way we ourselves would in similar circumstances—we are likely to misconstrue the situation. This is why we can't forget that the reactions of other people, like our own, are conditioned by their complex personal histories. And that no two personal histories are identical. Whenever we presuppose a symmetry of emotional landscapes between ourselves and our lover, we neglect the singularity of both.

4

The line between healthy curiosity and neurotic overinterpretation is sometimes extremely fine. It would be unethical to make no effort to understand our lover. Sometimes people use the idea that others are unknowable as an excuse to stop trying to empathize with their point of view. For instance, when men say that women are mystifying, they usually mean that they can't be bothered to try to close the gap between themselves and a particular woman. Along the same lines, it may be tempting to use the realization that we can't crack another person's cryptogram as a screen for the fact that we really don't care enough to make a genuine effort. Yet it's equally crucial to admit that we'll never fully penetrate the depths of those we love. And that our efforts to do so can become too insistent. In this sense, it's only when we learn to take a step back—when we learn to curb the urgency of our will to know—that we become capable of genuine emotional generosity.

Tolerating love's murky stretches demands patience in the face of the unknown. But the reward for this patience is, often, renewed passion. When two lovers choose to honor a space of unknowability between themselves, they preserve the sovereignty of both. They protect their ability to develop in independent directions. As a result, they nurture their continued capacity to replenish their relationship with fresh energies; they keep their alliance alive by making sure that each of them has something new to bring to it.

Anyone who has ever been in a long-distance relationship has had a taste of this. As difficult as it may be to be apart, periods of separation keep the romance interesting. They keep the lovers from collapsing into each other. And they also push aside the trivia of everyday life. When two lovers come together after a separation, they tend to focus on what is significant. They don't waste their time talking about the tedium of dry-cleaning, house-cleaning, car-cleaning, or teeth-cleaning. Rather, they feed their love with topics that are fundamentally worth talking about.

It's not work that keeps love alive; it's space. Space that we fill with fascinating things. This space, obviously, needs to be supplemented by other things such as kindness and trustworthiness. And it cannot get so vast that we lose our connection to our lover. There are times when we need the comforts of closeness, and others when we urgently want the energizing jolt of fusion. But if the relationship is to flourish in the long run, fusion needs to be offset by separation.

When we are too close to something, it's hard to see it properly. We can't make out the entire mountain when we're standing at its foot. Likewise, it's impossible to communicate with someone who is standing an inch away (unless, of course, you're having sex). Preserving some distance between self and other makes better communication possible. And it feeds desire over time. When we think that we know everything about our lover, he may cease to intrigue us. In contrast, when something about him remains slightly out of reach, we keep reaching for it.

Above I chose to highlight a scenario that many of us find more threatening than most other relationship disasters—the one where our lover unexpectedly wants out. I did so because I think that there's no greater test of our respect for our lover's nonnegotiable autonomy than letting him leave without protest when that's what he needs to do. This is one of the greatest gifts—one of the greatest acts of love—that we could ever give him. Love is bighearted. It wants what is best for the loved one. If it turns out that what is best for him doesn't involve us, we must accept this. This is tough, for sure. And there are more or less productive ways to end a relationship. If your lover picks fights, cheats on you, or disparages you in the hope that this will induce you to insist on a separation, he's being manipulative. However, if he candidly tells you that his feelings have shifted, there's no space for argument. You can't blame him. It's possible that he'll later regret his decision. In that case, he'll come back to you unprompted. But your attempts to convince him to stay will only alienate him more. Who, after all, wants to be with a woman who is so desperate for a relationship that she's willing to settle for a guy who has told her that he no longer wants her?

When a man needs to break things off, it's usually not because he's out to hurt you. He often wishes he could feel differently—that he could give you the love you want. He's unlikely to be withholding emotions that would save the relationship. The worst you could do, therefore, would be to try to convince him that he's mistaken. He knows he's not. And your efforts to prove him wrong will get you nowhere. The noblest thing you can do is to show appreciation for the fact that he was honest with you—that he had the guts to tell you how he feels. This is a sign that he esteems you enough to think that you deserve his frankness. And to the degree that you only want love that is freely given, you'll thank him for having spared you the indignity of staying in a relationship where your partner was merely pretending to love you. What could be more mortifying than discovering that your lover has stuck around only because he's too afraid to tell you the truth?

5

In the beginning of this book, I stated that you can't control what happens; you can only control how you respond to what happens. A breakup is one of the most obvious examples of this. There is, however, one thing that makes a big difference, namely the kind of man you have chosen to date. If you have selected one of the knuckle-draggers that many self-help guides seem so eager to sell you, I wouldn't necessarily expect an honest ending. These are the guys who will suddenly disappear on you without an explanation. Or drag you through the mud for months because they want you to be the one to pull the plug. That way, their conscience is clear no matter how badly they have offended you. They want you to bear the burden of ending the relationship because they're too spineless to do it themselves.

This has happened to me once—with Mr. Hyde. This is why he is the only one of my ex-partners I regret. This man went to astonishing lengths to dodge accountability. If I hung around as long as I did, it was primarily because I had trouble believing that any man could approach a relationship with as little integrity. Toward the end, it almost became an anthropological experiment for me. I was trying to wrap my head around the fact that men like him actually exist in the twenty-first century. I had read about them. But in my two decades of dating I had never come across one before.

My parting with Mr. Hyde was acrimonious. This wasn't because I couldn't tolerate the loss of his love. It was because I couldn't tolerate the idea of a man like him. I now know that my main mistake with him was to consent to date him in the first place. Ironically, I hesitated. In the initial stages, I kept thinking that he just wasn't that right for me. He seemed too traditionally "manly"—too controlling and self-centered. I got into the relationship at the urging of a friend who told me to reach beyond my comfort zone. This comfort zone consists of modern men who take it for granted that women are their equals. These are guys who don't waste their brains on trying to figure out how women differ from men. They treat women like human beings. Consequently, when they need to break up with one, they do so with a degree of decency. It wouldn't occur to them to resort to one of the stereotypical masculine escape hatches. What my experience with Mr. Hyde taught me is that my comfort zone is a fabulous place to date. When you opt for men who value women, love is just better. A hundred times better! These guys may still break your heart, of course. But they won't hurt you just to take you down.

My point here is that the kind of man you choose to date is the most important factor in your love life. Granted, it can be hard to read a man accurately right away. The unknowability I just talked about makes it impossible to make foolproof judgment calls. But there are usually early warning signs. It's a good idea to pay attention to these. This is among the things that you *can* control in a relationship.

One of the main reasons I have spent so much time trying to convince you that gender stereotypes are an atrocious basis for romance is that I think that guys who buy into such stereotypes are much more likely to mistreat you than guys who don't. As I noted in Chapter 2, a man who tells you that it's in men's "nature" to sleep around, flee from commitment, get unnerved by emotions, or idolize youth and beauty is prone to use these sentiments as an excuse to do exactly these things. He'll tell you that he can't help himself—that you should have more sympathy for what it means to be a man. *Forget that!* This kind of reasoning gives men permission to act dishonorably. It basically gives them the green light to hurt you. This is not to say that guys who don't adhere to this reasoning won't ever injure you. It's just that they know better than to try to justify their lapses by recourse to some universal "male psyche." They're much more likely to be straight with you—and to accept their share of responsibility for relationship failures.

That was the lesson of the first half of this book. I wanted to show that the "boys will be boys" mentality of our culture is designed to serve the interests of certain kinds of men— the kind you don't want to date. The lesson of the second half is that one of our most demanding tasks is to navigate the treacherous balance between staying open to love and being able to let go of it when necessary. Our biggest challenge is to love generously even when we have no way of knowing how things will evolve.

I've attempted to demonstrate that relationships that are built on the understanding that love is capricious are hardier than ones based on the expectation of stability. Such relationships are able to sustain a lot of damage without being permanently shattered. They admit uncertainty as part of the covenant of love. Partners in such relationships don't retreat at the first sign of trouble. They understand that moments of dissonance can be a part of love rather than a sign of its undoing. Sometimes love lags behind. Sometimes it just needs time to catch up. Lovers who are willing to wait and see know this.

Lovers who treat their relationship as a work-in-progress have a better chance of long-standing happiness than those who try to pin passion into a promise that neither party has the power to uphold. Although we can promise fidelity to our partner, we can't promise love. We can't know how we'll feel in the future. And we can't command ourselves to feel in a particular way. To promise to love someone for the rest of our lives is in some ways always a hollow promise. This doesn't mean that we won't ever be able to love in this way. Many people do. I hope you'll be one of them. It's just that we can never *guarantee* it.

If we truly respect the mystery of love, we won't pledge allegiance to its permanence. Rather, we'll pledge allegiance to our faithful efforts to stay open to its transformative energies. Such openness is, in the final analysis, our best defense against love's unexpected swerves. It keeps us from getting intimidated by love's detours, no matter how random these may seem. As such, it allows us to build more satisfying relationships. Its boldness protects us from those of love's failures that are due to sheer faintheartedness. This is why I think that we might be better off if, instead of promising everlasting love, we promised everlasting openness. Perhaps, then, we would have more honesty. And, thus, more love.

....

The Line in the Sand

A summary of what I've argued in this book might read as follows: "Relax. Let love happen. Forget about the games of romance. Be willing to risk everything. Let passion be your guide. But know when to walk away. You might get wounded and that's nothing to be frightened of. You might get disillusioned but that's not the end of the world. But still, *know when to walk away*."

The flipside of not being afraid to fall in love is not being afraid to leave a dead-end relationship. When you're not terrified of romantic disappointments, you're able to abandon an alliance that doesn't meet your needs. Or that hurts you in some way. You're able to draw that line in the sand. Your hand won't waver. The line will be clear and resolute. You'll be able to see it from an airplane two miles up in the sky. Staying on the right side of this line will protect you from substandard relationships. And it will save you from men who make you feel small and rejected. Whenever things cease to satisfy you, knowing where the line is will help you pick up your belongings and go looking for something better. This is a tremendously powerful position to be in.

I've spent a lot of time telling you that love is beyond your control. That passion is inherently unruly. That the likelihood of getting hurt is high. That you can't truly love without risking yourself. And that what is meant to happen will always find a way of happening. In part, I've done so in order to counteract our self-help culture's addiction to the idea that romance should come with safety nets and parachutes. And, in part, I've done so to convince you that a love failure is not the same thing as a life failure—that there are times when a so-called "failure" is the best way to end a relationship. I've pointed out that some of our most life-altering insights reach us through love's anguished endings. And I've illustrated that our efforts to domesticate romance are bound to fail even as they drain love of its vitality. None of this, however, is meant to imply that you should stay in a bad romance.

Your passion is too precious to be wasted on a relationship that weakens you. You don't have the power to control love. But you do have the power to decide what kinds of intimate scenarios you're willing to put up with; you have the power to rule out certain kinds of men. Most importantly, you have the power to call a loss a loss. Admittedly, being able to do so gracefully is something that few of us ever fully master. Often we fumble and make mistakes. We stay longer than we should. Or we fail to make a clean break, leaving too many loose ends. Knowing when and how to walk out of a problematic relationship is a skill we can only ever aspire to approximate. Yet we can definitely make progress. So I suppose that, in the end, even I have a rule: *Stay when love enriches you; leave when it doesn't.* Simple. But effective.

What's *not* effective is trying to turn yourself into someone you're not. The self-help culture I've been critiquing makes strong women paranoid about being strong. It strives to convince us that we can only succeed in love if we consent to play the game according to rules that were devised for a totally different era. This brainwashes us into thinking that there's something wrong with who and what we are. We start to second-guess ourselves, with the result that we dilute the independent spirit that makes modern women so amazing. We squander our strength in perfecting our romantic strategies when we should be focusing on developing well-rounded identities. We obsess about handling romance correctly when we should be building the foundations of our lives so that we have something solid to fall back on regardless of how our romantic destinies unfold. In the process, we sometimes inadvertently destroy the very spark that makes us interesting to quality men in the first place. We end up dating guys who fit the self-help model, namely macho guys who like to think of themselves as fearless hunters and who treat us accordingly. These guys may be glad to rescue us from spiders, but they'll never love us as their equals.

Many of our grandmothers and mothers trapped themselves in loveless marriages and sacrificed their talents for the sake of their husbands. We are fortunate to be the inheritors of a more egalitarian climate. It's for this reason that I find our self-help culture so alarming. This culture is trying to persuade us that the gains we have made as women—the very gains that have given us freedom—are somehow a barrier to our romantic success.

I don't think that it's coincidental that, at the very moment in history when women have achieved so much in other aspects of life, we have self-help authors telling us that men don't like independent women. Men supposedly want women to be a little helpless and incompetent. Don't believe a word of it. I've never met a man who prefers a helpless and incompetent woman over a strong and competent one. Most men are not the backward cavemen that self-help guides make them out to be. While such men do still exist, they're a dying breed. In this sense, men are not our enemy. Our self-help culture is. It's manipulating us into believing that to be lovable is to be the very antithesis of the modern woman.

There's nothing more insidious than this. There's nothing more sinister than implying that the very things that make women successful are also what make them undesirable. Our culture holds the specter of singleness over our heads, telling us that if we don't buy into traditional gender stereotypes, we won't end up getting married; we'll miss out on love. Again, don't believe a word of it. My experience has been that those women who don't compromise on their independence are the ones who end up with the best relationships. They find men who respect and admire them. They couple up with passionate men who are not afraid to show their feelings. They attract supportive men who don't hesitate to carry their share of the burden when things get dicey. Because these women manage to sidestep the snares of our self-help culture, they also manage to steer clear of men who need to denigrate women in order to prop up their sense of manliness. These women don't deceive men. They treat men as their friends. And men respond in kind.

It's easy to be swayed by the idea that we need to approach our love lives with the strategic acumen of a decorated general. Step-by-step programs are so enticing because they promise to make love more manageable. Many of us turn to them because, frankly, they're less intimidating than the intricacies of real love and real loss. They're a welcome distraction from the process of mourning a painful breakup. And they seduce us into thinking that we can learn to do things better the next time around. It's a lot easier to read a book that outlines the tenets of romantic success than to face the idea that human emotions are hardly ever clear-cut or straightforward. It's easier to digest the hundred best dating tips than to accept the prospect of having to navigate a complex relationship between two extraordinarily complex individuals.

The problem is that easy-fix strategies don't actually fix anything. All they do is leave us completely unprepared for those times when the rules don't yield the results we expect. Playing hard to get was supposed to win your guy's undying adoration? But instead he's pulling back! Not calling him for a week was supposed to bring him begging at your doorstep? But he's headed out of town instead. Pretending that you don't know how to change the light bulb was supposed to make him protective? But instead he tells you that he's looking for a sensible woman who is able to handle the minutiae of daily life. Praising his parallel parking skills was supposed to massage his ego? Instead, he wonders if you've bumped your head—can't you see what a shoddy job he's done!? Asking him to calculate the tip of your dinner bill was supposed to make him feel manly and competent? But instead he starts talking about his amazing ex who could do advanced calculus in her head.

What's so tragic about much of self-help advice is that it keeps us from doing the real work of learning how to relate to lovers in meaningful ways—ways that can endure moments of despair and murkiness as well as of joy and pleasure. It causes us to pour our energies into the most superficial aspects of romance, such as who is supposed to call whom first and when it's safe to admit that we know how to wield a hammer. This can cause us to overlook the much more difficult challenge of growing into lovers who are able to work through the sadder shades of romance.

We all know that the trials of love do not end at the altar. The perfect wedding dress doesn't always result in a perfect marriage. Nor do our "issues" magically disappear once we have made a commitment. Why, then, are so many us willing to believe that winning the game is the only thing that matters? Why do we let ourselves be pacified by the idea that if we follow the rules, we won't get hurt?

When I sat down to write this book, I told myself that there would be no rules. That I would produce an anti-self-help treatise of sorts. I wouldn't promise any easy fixes. Instead,

I would demonstrate that love will always outwit our fixes. It will always overflow the boundaries that we raise to enclose it. It's in the basic nature of love to be temperamental. Our era is trying to deny this. It's trying to turn love into something that's rationally controllable. I hope I've convinced you of the foolishness of this endeavor. Not only is it doomed to fail, but it cheats romance of its enchantment. It turns love into just another page in our investment portfolio. Supposedly, the more prudently we invest, the higher the profits. But, actually, the opposite is the case. In love, it's those who take the biggest risks who reap the biggest gains. Sometimes they lose everything. But when they win, they win the jackpot.

So, no rules. But here are some potent anti-rules to hold up to the self-help vampires lurking in the shadows:

1. *Stop trying so hard.* Give up your efforts to force love into a self-help cast. It will never fit, no matter how much you struggle. The only thing you'll achieve are blisters in your brain. And love is not a Rubik's Cube either. You can't solve its riddles by clicking the red, blue, green, yellow, etc., pieces neatly into place. You'll only get blisters on your fingers. So give yourself the heavenly permission to let love do the heavy lifting all by itself. Not only will this feel great, but it will save you a fortune in therapist and manicure fees.

2. *Stop being so cautious.* Love is one of those human experiences where caution is overrated. If you want to be safe,

go shopping at Zara with your best friend. The worst that can happen to you there is that you won't be able to resist the adorable little black dress on sale. But when it comes to love, don't expect caution to get you anywhere. Applying caution to love is like driving uphill with your emergency brake on. You might be able to keep going for a while, but eventually, you'll need to find a mechanic.

3. *Stop analyzing your every move.* The more time you spend analyzing your love life, the less time you'll have left for loving. You'll give yourself a splitting headache. So save yourself the trouble and don't try to think it through. Except, of course, when you start to get that sinking feeling in the pit of your stomach that tells you that something is seriously wrong. If you begin to feel injured, damaged, offended, or nauseated, feel free to think yourself right out the door.

4. *Stop expecting your guy to act like a caveman.* Unless, of course, you're ready to be dragged through the city streets by your hair. The great thing is that when you stop insisting that your guy is the direct descendant of an ape, you might end up with someone as glossy as *Gossip Girl*'s Nate. Okay. Maybe not the actual Nate. But someone who is willing to furrow his brow, flash a smile, and chatter away just like the real one.

5. *Stop apologizing for being strong.* This one is worth repeating like a mantra: Stop apologizing for being strong and self-sufficient. Men worth dating are much more likely to want precisely these qualities than artificial displays of feminine neediness. There isn't much that's more pathetic than guys who need to put women down in order to convince themselves of their masculine valor. Who needs these guys?

6. *Stop being afraid to have needs and vulnerabilities.* Being strong doesn't mean that you're Supergirl, or even Lois Lane. You have needs. You have vulnerabilities. You even have episodes of hopelessness. You have moments when you want a strong shoulder to lean on. But so does your guy. Having someone compassionate to turn to during times of breakdown is worth more than Superman's red cape. Your guy knows this as well as you do. That's why he's with you.

7. *Stop running after guys who don't want you.* There's no point in pursuing a reluctant man. You'll only get a cramp in your side. And then your heart starts to hurt. You'll lose your confidence. You'll begin to doubt your desirability. You'll get your hair done so often that half of it falls out. Your friends start plotting an intervention. Before they get to it, it's time to stage your own. If you need to fly to Moscow to stop chasing that guy, do so. You absolutely deserve a man who meets you halfway.

8. *Stop looking for a guy without issues.* Everyone has issues. And guys with some complicated ones are often more interesting than those whose main issue is choosing the right pair of loafers in the morning. Do you require yourself to be completely free of issues—completely devoid of doubts, anxieties, insecurities, uncertainties, and ambivalences? No? So I thought. Why, then, would you expect your guy to be like a newborn babe with no history or human hesitation?

9. *Stop manipulating the guy you love.* Focus on building a complex character. Make some money. Get going with your career. Learn Italian. Take up cross-country skiing. Bake five thousand cookies. Hand them out to everyone from your boss to the cute FedEx delivery guy. If you need a project, treat your life like a work of art. Try to make a masterpiece out of it. But don't do this to the guy you're dating. Once he realizes that you've turned your relationship into a papier-mâché project, he'll resent you. A lot.

10. *Stop regretting every false step you ever took.* It's hard to get things right in love. People get hurt. You get hurt. You end up hurting your guy. No matter how much you try to protect yourself from such mishaps, they happen. They happen if you're actually loving rather than just playing house with someone you kind of like. Missing your step, and even missing your way, is part of love's reality. It forces you to reassess the path you're on. It asks you to

make some modifications. This is its way of shaping your soul.

11. *Stop thinking of loss as a pure loss.* Keep in mind that we rarely lose valuable things without getting something in return. The payback may be slow in coming. And sometimes it's hard to even recognize it as such. But if you wait long enough, even the worst loss is likely to bring a compensation. If nothing else, it purifies your character so that when the next hot guy comes along, you'll have enough charisma to magnetize him. He'll be so smitten that he'll fly you to Tahiti on a vacation for two. You'll pay for the hotel room, of course. You're not a charity case. Not you.

Was that twelve of them? No? Only eleven? Well, this one deserves double-billing: *Stop trying so hard.* There you go. These are your twelve anti-rules. They won't guarantee your everlasting happiness. They won't even guarantee a ring on your finger. And, alas, they definitely won't guarantee that Tom Welling will super-speed to your side when the going gets tough. But they'll guarantee that you will have lived. Boldly. Bravely. Audaciously. Like a true lover.

NOTES
....

INTRODUCTION

The academic texts from my Harvard syllabus have influenced my thinking in this book. I list them here in the order in which I taught them (or selections from them): Plato, *The Symposium* (New York: Penguin Classics, 2003); Jelaluddin Rumi, *The Book of Love: Poems of Ecstasy and Longing* (New York: HarperOne, 2003); Simone de Beauvoir, *The Second Sex* (New York: Vintage, 1989); Sigmund Freud, *Five Lectures on Psychoanalysis* (London: W. W. Norton & Co., 1990); Jacques Lacan, *The Seminar of Jacques Lacan, Book XX: On Feminine Sexuality, the Limits of Love and Knowledge* (New York: W. W. Norton & Co., 1999); Karen Horney, *Feminine Psychology* (New York: W. W. Norton & Co., 1993); Roland Barthes, *A Lover's Discourse: Fragments* (New York: Hill & Wang, 1979); Luce Irigaray, *To Be Two* (New York: Routledge, 2001); Julia Kristeva, *Tales of Love* (New York: Columbia University Press, 1987); Julia Kristeva, *Black Sun: Depression and Melancholia* (New York: Columbia University Press, 1989); Hélène Cixous, *"Coming to Writing" and Other Essays* (Cambridge,

MA: Harvard University Press, 1991); bell hooks, *All About Love* (New York: Harper, 2001); Thomas Mann, *Death in Venice* (New York: Vintage, 1989); Jane Austen, *Sense and Sensibility* (New York: Penguin Classics, 2003); Alice Walker, *By the Light of My Father's Smile* (New York: Ballantine Books, 1999); and Jeanette Winterson, *The Passion* (New York: Grove Press, 1997).

CHAPTER 1: SAVING THE SOUL OF LOVE

John Gray's *Men Are from Mars, Women Are from Venus: The Classic Guide to Understanding the Opposite Sex* (New York: Quill, 1992) created a cultural phenomenon that has had a huge impact on millions of women. Since 1992, Gray has published a dozen or so follow-up guides, all featuring the basic idea that many of our most tenacious romantic difficulties arise from the fact that men and women are fundamentally different. *Mars and Venus Starting Over: A Practical Guide for Finding Love Again After a Painful Breakup, Divorce, or the Loss of a Loved One* (New York: Quill, 2002) is one of these sequels.

Although Gray's books are often insightful, I'm resistant to his basic premise, for reasons that will become clear in the next couple of chapters. To put things simply, I'm not at all convinced that two women in a relationship would find things any easier than a man and a woman. If you swap your boyfriend for a girlfriend next week, I doubt your relationship problems will miraculously disappear. If you have trouble relating to your partner, it's not because he's a man, but because he's a person with a highly idiosyncratic character—one that isn't always immediately accessible to you (or even to him). People are too different from each other for us to assume that all men are one way and all women another way. This kind of thinking impoverishes our relationships because it causes us to relate to our partners through stereotypes that fail to capture the full complexity of who they are.

The sexual double standard that I refer to in this chapter has been with us at least since Adam and Eve. It penalizes women for being sexual creatures, implying that women are designed to resist sex and that those who enjoy it are somehow "loose" or defective. Even though the 1960s supposedly liberated us from this kind of thinking, it's actually strikingly strong right now. We have a crop of reformed bad boys and a former pimp writing relationship guides that tell women that the only way to romantic success is to keep their legs tightly crossed (some of these guides are listed in the following note). Barely concealed underneath the insistence that women's sexuality gets them in romantic trouble is a deeply misogynistic hatred and/or fear of female sexual power.

CHAPTER 2: MEN WHO ASK FOR DIRECTIONS MAKE BETTER LOVERS

I consulted the following self-help guides in preparation for writing this book (listed in the order of publication date): Connell Cowan and Melvyn Kinder, *Smart Women, Foolish Choices* (New York: Signet, 1986); Sherrie Schneider and Ellen Fein, *The Rules: Time-Tested Secrets for Capturing the*

Heart of Mr. Right (New York: Grand Central Publishing, 1995); Steven Carter and Julia Sokol, *Men Like Women Who Like Themselves* (New York: Dell Publishing, 1996); Carolyn N. Bushong, *The Seven Dumbest Relationship Mistakes Smart People Make* (New York: Villard, 1997); Sherry Argov, *Why Men Love Bitches: From Doormat to Dream girl—A Woman's Guide to Holding Her Own in a Relationship* (Avon, MA: Adams Media, 2002); Greg Behrendt and Liz Tuccillo, *He's Just Not That Into You: The No-Excuses Truth to Understanding Guys* (New York: Simon Stoplight Entertainment, 2004); Sherry Argov, *Why Men Marry Bitches: A Woman's Guide to Winning Her Man's Heart* (New York: Simon & Schuster, 2006); Big Boom, *If You Want Closure in Your Relationship, Start with Your Legs: A Guide to Understanding Men* (New York: Fireside, 2007); Bob Berkowitz, *What Men Won't Tell You but Women Need to Know* (New York: Harper Paperbacks, 2008); Marie Forleo, *Make Every Man Want You: Or Make Yours Want You More* (New York: McGraw-Hill, 2008); Steve Santagati, *The Manual: A True Bad Boy Explains How Men Think, Date, and Mate—and What Women Can Do to Come Out on Top* (New York: Three Rivers Press, 2008); Whitney Casey, *The Man Plan: Drive Men Wild...Not Away* (New York: Perigee Trade, 2009); Ash Green, *Sexy and Confident: How to Be the Dream girl Men Want, Have a Better Life, and Improve Your Self-Esteem* (New York: Artrum Media, 2009); Steve Harvey, *Act Like a Lady, Think Like a Man: What Men Really Think About Love, Relationships, Intimacy, and Commitment* (New York: Amistad, 2009); Romy Miller, *How to Be Wanted: Use the Law of Attraction to Date the Man You Most Desire and Live the Life You Deserve* (New York: The Book Factory, 2009). Some of these guides are much better than others. Not all advocate gender stereotypes. But most do.

Around the time I was polling my male friends about women and light bulbs, I mentioned in one of my emails to my friend Heather that I was tired of reading that men are programmed to stray and that women should pretend they don't know how to change the light bulb. Here is her response:

> I'm having a bit of trouble with the addition. Are women capable of straying in this terrible self-help world? Because, in my calculation, if men are the only ones doing the straying, this mathematically doesn't work! Are all of these helpless women who can't change light bulbs (but surely they can cook...god help us if they can't cook!)...are these women all just waiting (between fainting spells and broken fingernails) for these men to come to them after all those horrid light-bulb changers have ruined their manly protective instincts? Just a mathematical dilemma I'm seeing unfold...Warren and I change flat tires and light bulbs interchangeably. I should stop, shouldn't I? He's going to leave me any minute, isn't he? In fact...I'm going to leave this bag of recycling right here in the middle of my kitchen so he can take it out! Surely making him take out the garbage will restore his masculinity.

What's so amazing is that Heather knew immediately what kind of self-help advice I was dealing with. The manly man/helpless female model is so endemic in our culture that it has infiltrated our bloodstream without any conscious effort on our part. We inject it in the morning with our Special K. We sip it with our apple martinis. That darling little boy who is running a lemonade stand up the street? Watch out! His recipe: ¼ lemon juice, ¼ water, ¼ sugar, and ¼ female subordination.

CHAPTER 3: BAD SCIENCE CAN'T TELL US A DAMN THING ABOUT LOVE

The book I picked up at Chicago O'Hare is Leil Lowndes, *How to Make Anyone Fall in Love with You* (New York: McGraw-Hill, 1997).

Besides *Anatomy of Love: A Natural History of Mating, Marriage, and Why We Stray* (New York: Random House, 1992), Helen Fisher's books include *Why We Love: The Nature and Chemistry of Romantic Love* (New York: Henry Holt & Co., 2004) and *Why Him? Why Her?: Finding Real Love by Understanding Your Personality Type* (New York: Henry Holt & Co., 2009). Other works that promote the evolutionary perspective include David M. Buss, *The Evolution of Desire: Strategies of Human Mating* (New York: Basic Books, 2003) and Robin Baker, *Sperm Wars: Infidelity, Sexual Conflict, and Other Bedroom Battles* (New York: Basic Books, 2006).

The socially constructed nature of gender is so widely discussed (and so taken for granted) in contemporary gender studies that it would be impossible to name all the books in the field. I'll restrict myself to three classics: Judith Butler, *Gender Trouble: Feminism and the Subversion of Identity* (New York: Routledge, 1990); Judith Halberstam, *Female Masculinity* (Durham, NC: Duke University Press, 1998); and Anne Fausto-Sterling, *Sexing the Body: Gender Politics and the Construction of Sexuality* (New York: Basic Books, 2000).

Christina Konecny's paper is entitled "Breeding Grounds: Familial Desire and the (Hetero)normative Texture of Preschool Geographies." She's working on a Master's thesis on the same topic. She specifies that her analysis applies to most North American preschools that rely on interest areas (such as the "home" and "block" areas) to organize space. The following books offer a general introduction to gender and early education: Nicola Yelland, *Gender in Early Childhood* (New York: Routledge, 1998); Glenda MacNaughton, *Rethinking Gender in Early Childhood Education* (London: Paul Chapman, 2000); and Barrie Thorne, *Gender Play: Girls and Boys in School* (New Brunswick, NJ: Rutgers University Press, 1993).

The quote from Simone de Beauvoir is from *The Second Sex* (see Note to Introduction).

There is an episode of *Criminal Minds* (Season 4: "52 Pickup") that pushes the man-the-hunter notion to its limit. The Behavioral Analysis Unit of the FBI is investigating a series of gruesome murders committed by a man who finds his female victims by cruising crowded bars. The team discovers that the murderer most likely took a self-help class designed to teach men the art of picking up women. Agents

Morgan, Hotchner, and Prentiss visit the class. They watch from the sidelines while the instructor (named "Viper") gives a group of men the following advice: "Men are put on this earth to hunt women. And even though women deny it, they want to be hunted. They *need* it. It's part of our biological imperative as animals. And the competition the opposite sex puts you through, pitting you against other guys, against your own friends even, it's all to reassure themselves that they have brought home the best possible mate...My job is to help you slash past every defense...You may not have ribbed abs, or afford table service, but if you're smarter and more interesting, then you'll be a better predator. Because this is the jungle, my friends. And your prey *wants* to be caught." In the end of this, Morgan turns to Hotchner and Prentiss and says, "Will you listen to that language? He's training serial killers." Need I say more?

CHAPTER 4: FOR BETTER ROMANTIC ADVICE, WATCH *GOSSIP GIRL*

A lot of new work in media studies has focused on how contemporary television shows are negotiating a new gendered reality. Here are a handful of books I've used in my courses: Roz Kaveney, *Teen Dreams: Reading Teen Film and Television from "Heathers" to "Veronica Mars"* (London: I. B. Tauris, 2006); Janet McCabe and Kim Akass (eds.), *Quality TV: Contemporary American Television & Beyond* (London: I. B. Tauris, 2007); Glyn Davis and Kay Dickinson (eds.), *Teen TV: Genre, Consumption, and Identity* (London: British

Film Institute, 2008); Mark Jancovich and James Lyon (eds.), *Quality Popular Television: Cult TV, the Industry, and Fans* (London: British Film Institute, 2008); and Sharon Marie Ross and Louisa Ellen Stein (eds.), *Teen Television: Essays on Programming and Fandom* (Jefferson, NC: McFarland, 2008).

On famous lovers who knew how to long for each other, see Cristina Nehring, *A Vindication of Love: Reclaiming Romance for the Twenty-first Century* (New York: Harper, 2009). I also like Nehring's book for its endorsement of the idea that passion is not meant to be safe or controllable.

CHAPTER 5: MODERN CINDERELLAS LOOK BEYOND THE PRINCE'S BALL

In anticipation of my discussion in Chapter 7, I want to emphasize that men don't have a monopoly on narcissism. Women can fall into equally toxic modes of relating. We can be just as keen to use relationships to give meaning to our existence. The more empty our lives feel, the more likely we are to expect our partner to boost our sense of self. The problem is that doing so blocks everything that is transformative about love. Normally, love adds fresh ingredients to our emotional repertoire. It asks us to develop through an encounter with a person who is completely different from us—a person who allows us to see the world via an unfamiliar lens. Lovers who are overly narcissistic frustrate this process. They are reluctant to meet what philosophers call "the altogether other"—the point of radical otherness in another person that cannot be tamed or gentrified. Instead of welcoming what is genuinely "other" about their partners, they try to neutralize this otherness. They try to erase all indications that their partner is different from the fantasy they have fashioned. As a result, they miss out on the expansion of personality that only a courageous brush with "the altogether other" would make possible.

On the "altogether other," see Emmanuel Levinas, *Entre Nous: Thinking-of-the-Other* (New York: Columbia University Press, 2000).

"The Sandman" can be found in E. T. A. Hoffmann, *The Sandman and Other Stories* (Gloucester, UK: Dodo Press, 2008). Freud wrote a famous analysis of the story in his essay "The Uncanny." Freud's text can be found in *The Uncanny* (New York: Penguin Classics, 2003).

Judy's statement in *Vertigo* comes from this bit of dialogue:

Judy: Couldn't you like me, just me the way I am? When we first started out, it was so good; we had fun. And...and then you started in on the clothes. Well, I'll wear the darn clothes if you want me to, if, if you'll just, just like me.

Scottie: The color of your hair...

Judy: Oh, no!

Scottie: Judy, please, it can't matter to you.

Judy: If I let you change me, will that do it? If I do what you tell me, will you love me?

Scottie: Yes. Yes.

Judy: All right. All right then, I'll do it. I don't care anymore about me.

The dialogue deftly captures the gist of what it means to turn a woman into a fantasy object.

CHAPTER 6: WHY PLAYING HARD TO GET WON'T WORK

Laura Kipnis's *Against Love: A Polemic* (New York: Vintage, 2003) is a hard-hitting critique of our culture's denigration of singleness. My friend and colleague at the University of Toronto, Michael Cobb, is writing a wonderful book on the topic entitled *Single: Lonely, Impossible, Empty, and Alone* (forthcoming from NYU Press).

CHAPTER 7: IT'S ALL ABOUT THE THING

Lacan talks about the Thing (or *das Ding*, as he often calls it) throughout his work, but the most sustained analysis may be in *The Seminar of Jacques Lacan, Book VII: The Ethics of Psychoanalysis* (New York: W. W. Norton & Co., 1992). The concept of "more than" can be found in *The Seminar of Jacques Lacan, Book XI: The Four Fundamental Concepts of Psychoanalysis* (New York: W. W. Norton & Co., 1981). Here are the names of some of the leading Lacanian scholars: Joan Copjec, Bruce Fink, Roberto Harari, Lewis Kirshner, Eric Santner, Kaja Silverman, Luke Thurston, Slavoj Žižek, and Alenka Zupančič. The field is notoriously difficult, even for professional academics, so I don't recommend any of these authors for beach reading.

Jean-Paul Sartre's most famous work is *Being and Nothingness* (New York: Washington Square Press, 1993). The title more or less says it all: At the heart of "Being" is "Nothingness."

CHAPTER 8: SEEING THE EXTRAORDINARY
WITHIN THE ORDINARY

My thinking in this chapter has benefited from the work of Alenka Zupančič, particularly her brilliant *The Shortest Shadow: Nietzsche's Philosophy of the Two* (Cambridge, MA: The MIT Press, 2003).

Plato discusses the madness of love in *Phaedrus* (New York: Penguin Classics, 2005).

CHAPTER 9: BREAKING THE PATTERNS OF PAIN

Freud talks about the repetition compulsion throughout his work. For a general and highly accessible overview of his ideas, I recommend the following titles (all published by W. W. Norton & Co.): *Five Lectures in Psychoanalysis*, *The New Introductory Lectures in Psychoanalysis*, *The Interpretation of Dreams*, *Civilization and Its Discontents*, and *Beyond the Pleasure Principle*. Freud's theory of trauma and his discussion of the deadened "crust" can be found in *Beyond the Pleasure Principle*.

It would be impossible to name all the thinkers who have taken up Freud's ideas (and whose work has impacted mine). Here are some of the most pleasant to read: Christopher Bollas, Michael Eigen, Jonathan Lear, Juliet Mitchell, and Adam Phillips. From the early years of psychoanalysis, I would single out Melanie Klein, Hans Loewald, and D. W. Winnicott. And then there's of course Carl Gustav Jung, for those who are looking for a more mythological approach.

On shifting the blame, there are three self-help guides I like: Susan Forward, *Men Who Hate Women & The Women*

Who Love Them (New York: Bantam Books, 1986); Steven Carter and Julia Sokol, *Men Who Can't Love: How to Recognize a Commitmentphobic Man Before He Breaks Your Heart* (New York: E. Evans & Co., 1996); and Lundy Bancroft, *Why Does He Do That? Inside the Minds of Angry and Controlling Men* (New York: Berkeley Books, 2002). If these books are not on my most-wanted list for bad self-help advice, it's because they are excellent. They will be particularly helpful for any woman who suspects that she might be in an abusive relationship.

CHAPTER 10: A LOVE FAILURE IS NOT A LIFE FAILURE
Kant's discussion of the two ethical scenarios presented in the beginning of this chapter can be found in *Critique of Practical Reason* (Cambridge: Cambridge University Press, 1997). Lacan offers an analysis of Kant's scenarios in *The Ethics of Psychoanalysis* (see Note to Chapter 7). Žižek picks up the issue in *The Metastases of Enjoyment: Six Essays on Woman and Causality* (London: Verso, 2006). Zupančič, in turn, addresses it in *Ethics of the Real: Kant, Lacan* (New York: Verso, 2000).

CHAPTER 11: MOURNING WELL IS LIVING WELL
Freud's essay, "Mourning and Melancholia," can be found in Peter Gay (ed.), *The Freud Reader* (New York: W. W. Norton & Co., 1995). I also highly recommend Adam Phillips, *Darwin's Worms: On Life Stories and Death Stories* (New York: Basic Books, 2000).

Readers interested in trauma, including the idea that we can inherit the traumas of our parents, might benefit from the following works: Shoshana Felman and Dori Laub, *Testimony: Crises of Witnessing in Literature, Psychoanalysis, and History* (New York: Routledge, 1991); Cathy Caruth, *Unclaimed Experience: Trauma, Narrative, and History* (Baltimore, MD: The Johns Hopkins University Press, 1996); Dominick LaCapra, *Writing History, Writing Trauma* (Baltimore, MD: The Johns Hopkins University Press, 2000); Ruth Leys, *Trauma: A Genealogy* (Chicago: The University of Chicago Press, 2000); and E. Ann Kaplan, *Trauma Culture: The Politics of Terror and Loss in Media and Literature* (Piscataway, NJ: Rutgers University Press, 2005).

CHAPTER 12: WHAT IS MEANT TO HAPPEN ALWAYS WILL

One of the best books on the unpredictability of love is Stephen A. Mitchell, *Can Love Last? The Fate of Romance over Time* (New York: W. W. Norton & Co., 2002).

ABOUT THE AUTHOR

Photo by Bohdan Turok;
www.BohdanTurok.com

Mari Ruti was educated at Brown, Harvard, and the University of Paris. After finishing her Harvard doctorate in 2000, she spent four years as assistant director of the university's program for the Study of Women, Gender, and Sexuality. She is currently associate professor of critical theory at the University of Toronto English Department, where she teaches contemporary theory, continental philosophy, psychoanalysis, gender studies, and popular culture. Ruti is the author of two academic books: *Reinventing the Soul: Posthumanist Theory and Psychic Life* (New York: Other Press, 2006) and *A World of Fragile Things: Psychoanalysis and the Art of Living* (Albany, NY: SUNY Press, 2009). She splits her time between Toronto, the East Coast, and Maui.